The New
Needlecraft
Project Book

The New Needlecraft Project Book

Over 60 inspired embroidery, needlepoint, patchwork, quilting, appliqué, knitting and crochet projects

Lucinda Ganderton

Photographs by James Duncan

SMITHMARK

For my sister, Emma, with love.

This edition published in 1996 by
SMITHMARK Publishers Inc, a division of US Media Holdings Inc,
16 East 32nd Street, New York, NY 10016.

SMITHMARK books are available for bulk purchase for sales
promotion and for premium use.
For details write or call the Manager of Special Sales, SMITHMARK Publishers Inc,
16 East 32nd Street, New York, NY 10016: (212) 532-6600.

ISBN 0-8317-7338-3

Produced by Anness Publishing Limited
Hermes House, 88-89 Blackfriars Road, London SE1 8HA

Printed In Singapore by Star Standard Industries Pte. Ltd.

1 3 5 7 9 10 8 6 4 2

Publisher's Note
Please note that all templates and charts referred to in this book
are set out together on pages 114 to 127.

Previously published as part of a larger compendium, *The Complete Guide to Needlecraft*.

Measurements
Both imperial and metric measurements have been given in the text.
Where conversions produced an awkward number, these have been rounded
for convenience, but will produce an accurate result if one system is
followed throughout.

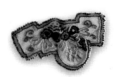

Contents

INTRODUCTION   6

EMBROIDERY   8
Projects   10

NEEDLEPOINT   34
Projects   36

PATCHWORK AND QUILTING   48
Projects   50

APPLIQUÉ   64
Projects   66

KNITTING   82
Projects   84

CROCHET   100
Projects   102

TEMPLATES   114

INDEX   128

CONVERSION TABLES   128

Introduction

Traditional needlecrafts form an essential part of our lives and have been carried on throughout the world for centuries in their many forms. In the past, sewing skills were a very necessary part of running a household. Clothing had to be made and patched, socks needed to be darned and domestic linen repaired. It was only the leisured classes who could indulge in the more refined arts of delicate embroidery, white crochet lace or ornate crazy patchwork, as a way of passing the long hours and to show off their skills. For most women needlecrafts were part of the daily routine or a means of earning a living.

Domestic needlework in the early twentieth century was dominated by dressmaking and hand knitting, but society has changed immensely since then. Recent years have seen a major

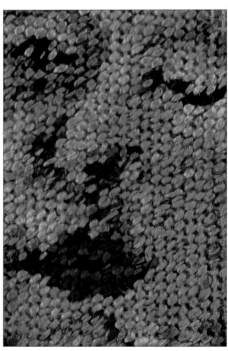

The expert dollmaker who created this striking punk figure constructed the doll's garments from fabric made by the newest machine embroidery techniques.

This multimedia collage uses stitching and colour to bold effect.

revival of interest in all types of decorative and functional needlecraft. There has been a proliferation of craft manuals and magazines, and a plethora of materials is now available from specialist suppliers.

It seems that we are all seeking an escape from the mass produced uniformity of shop-bought products. Even the most basic knowledge of how to sew can enable us to personalize clothing, create original gifts for friends and family, or stitch soft furnishings to make our homes more distinctive and individual.

This book is intended both as a guide to long-established crafts and as an introduction to new and creative ways of working through practical projects. Its six chapters in turn cover embroidery, needlepoint, patchwork and quilting, appliqué, knitting and

crochet. The projects cover a wonderful range of decorative and useful items to create from samplers, curtains and cushion covers to mobiles, baby gifts, hats and jewel boxes. However simple the technique employed, and no matter how quick and easy the item is to make, you will be delighted to find that each project is a challenging, highly attractive and stylish piece of work.

The sixty-five projects, designed by leading crafts people, are aimed at both the experienced needleworker and the complete beginner. Some of them are

The emotional impact of embroidery is illustrated by this expressive rendering of a woman's face in tent stitch on canvas.

Needlepoint cushions (pillows) have been popular since the eighteenth century; this modern design is based on the imagery of Indian decoration.

uses. The recent development of materials such as water-soluble fabrics, metallic threads and iron-on fusible bondings mean that ideas can now find even more new and innovative expression.

There is a vast international field of various needlecrafts to draw ideas and inspiration from, and many reference books devoted to topics that are dealt with here in a few pages. *The New Needlecraft Project Book* provides a fantastic collection of projects which will develop the skills of new needle-workers, test the talents of competent crafters, and inspire and stimulate even the most advanced practitioners.

quick to do and can be made in an afternoon; others are more complex and offer a longer term challenge. All the projects are carefully explained with easy to follow step-by-step photographs, and all the necessary templates, charts and patterns are included at the back of the book.

Embroiderers, quiltmakers and knitters have always been inventive. All sewing was done by hand until the arrival of the sewing machine in the l870s. This was welcomed as a relief from the tedium of straight seaming, but its decorative applications were immediately recognized. The swing needle, or zigzag machine has opened up new ways of embroidering which are still being explored. Over the centuries, unusual items such as shells, feathers, ribbons and even hair and iridescent beetle wings have been incorporated with velvets, silks, beads and sequins to create decorative works, and all kinds of yarns and fabrics have been adapted to sometimes unexpected

Contemporary designers are breaking down the boundaries between embroidery and other crafts. This vase of flowers combines the precision of machine stitching with randomly torn coloured paper.

Embroidery

Embroidery, or the use of decorative stitchery, is an ancient craft which can be reinterpreted in a highly personal style today. The possibilities for combining threads and stitches are endless, and almost any fabric or garment can be embroidered either by hand or machine. The exciting projects in this section include original accessories for the home and items to wear, to keep or to give as presents.

Alphabet Sampler

In the 1800s, schoolteachers and private governesses would combine the teaching of literacy and needlecraft by giving their pupils – both boys and girls – the painstaking task of embroidering a cross stitch sampler. Surviving antique examples, by children as young as six, sometimes exhibit remarkably accomplished sewing skills. Specially printed pattern books were used as a guide and this lower-case alphabet first appeared in a French publication at the turn of the nineteenth century.

MATERIALS
25cm (10in) square of 14-count white Aida cloth
Stranded embroidery threads in burgundy, scarlet, burnt orange, yellow gold and olive green
Embroidery scissors
20cm (8in) square wooden picture frame with glass
Fabric marker pen

1 The layout of the alphabet used here is for a 15cm (6in) square, but it could easily be adapted to fit a rectangular shape. Allowing a 5cm (2in) margin, work the first A in the top left corner, using three strands of burgundy thread. Be sure that all the cross stitches lie in the same direction. Finish off the first colour and, with scarlet thread, work the B. Use burnt orange, yellow gold, then olive green for the next letters and continue working the alphabet, keeping the same sequence of colours in each row.

2 Press the finished embroidery lightly from the back. Place the glass from the frame on to the right side and centre the design. Cut a piece of card to fit the frame, fold the edges of the fabric around the card and lace tightly at the back.

Potpourri Bag

S imple checked fabric has long been produced in many parts of the world and is a favourite choice for household textiles. This homespun cotton potpourri bag is inspired by the functional hand-woven cloth made by the American Shaker community. Its square weave forms a good basis for the counted threads of cross stitch and the contrasting heart motif fits neatly into the blue and white squared pattern. The natural texture of the raffia tie gives the finished bag a country-style appeal.

MATERIALS
23 x 33cm (9 x 13in) piece of checked fabric
Stranded embroidery thread in dark pink
Matching cotton sewing thread
Dressmaker's pins
Potpourri, lavender flowers or
  sweet-scented dried herbs
Length of garden raffia

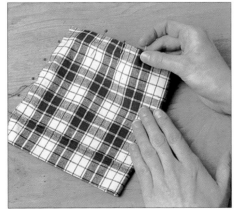

1 Following the chart given, embroider three cross stitch hearts, spaced evenly along one half of one long edge of the fabric. Use three strands of the thread and work over three or four threads of fabric, depending on the size of the weave. Make sure that the stitches are all worked in the same direction.

2 Fold the short edges together, with the embroidery on the inside. Pin together the short edges, and the bottom (with embroidery). Hand or machine stitch, leaving a 12mm (½in) seam allowance. Fold the open top edge over and hem on the wrong side.

3 Clip the corners, then turn the bag right side out and press lightly. Fill the bag with potpourri, lavender flowers or sweet-scented dried herbs. Tie a length of raffia around the top of the bag to make a decorative bow. Make a hanging loop from another, shorter length of raffia.

Cross Stitch Motifs

Counted cross stitch motifs are quick to work, easy to adapt and can be mounted in a variety of ways to make personalized presents for all occasions. Specialist manufacturers produce an interesting range of items designed to display lace or small pieces of embroidery. These include boxes, powder bowls (jars), Christmas-tree decorations, jewellery and glass paperweights. Greetings-card blanks are available in assorted shapes and sizes, including ones small enough to make gift tags.

Right: All the designs in this project are worked with three strands of embroidery thread on 12- or 14-count Aida cloth, which is woven specially for cross stitch work. It is more convenient to use than evenweave linen, as the individual threads of cloth do not have to be counted. Each symbol on the chart in the template section at the end of the book represents one cross-stitch.

1 By experimenting with different-coloured embroidery threads and background fabrics, strikingly varied interpretations of a single motif can be created. Aida cloth is available in a range of colours and can also be dyed using cold-water dyes. This design can be worked in dark green with two shades of pink as a romantic rose garland; in pale pink and light green to look like a wreath of apples; or in toning orange colours for a warm country feel.

2 The rose garland makes a perfect dressing-table ornament, when displayed on the lid of a crystal powder bowl (jar). Follow the supplier's instructions for assembling the various components and ensure that the motif lies centrally by lining it up with the lid before cutting it out.

3 The antique feel of the cast pewter frame complements the soft colours of the apple wreath, while the smooth gold adds extra warmth to the bright orange variation.

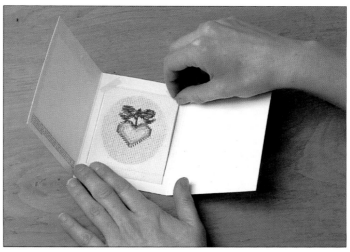

THE SCANDINAVIAN HEART is an ideal design for a Christmas card and could be worked as a single motif or repeated to create an all-over design.

TO MAKE A VALENTINE HEART CARD Some card blanks are produced with an adhesive area for mounting embroidery, but double-sided sticky tape is a good alternative for mounting work. Check that the design is aligned correctly in the space before gluing down the back of the cardboard.

Left: TO MAKE THE WOVEN HEART Work all the white areas first, before the red. Green fabric emphasizes the colour contrast, but a softer choice of threads would transform the design into a valentine heart.

THE WOVEN HEART The festive combination of red and white is a favourite choice in Norway, the source of this woven heart pattern.

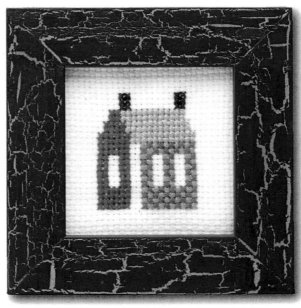

Right: THE LITTLE SCHOOLHOUSE design is adapted from an American quilting block. It would make an apt gift to welcome somebody to their new home.

Fabric Book

This fabric-covered book could be put to many uses: as a photo album containing pictures of a special event, as a sketchbook or as a notebook in which to write down favourite quotations and memories. The direct naive style of the birds and the tree is reminiscent of the Pennsylvania Dutch folk tradition, but the interpretation is fresh and contemporary.

Cotton fabrics with small-scale floral designs, sometimes known as "charm" prints and sold specifically for making patchwork, are best suited to this project.

MATERIALS
2 pieces of mounting board 23 x 28cm (9 x 11in)
Masking tape
2 sheets of watercolour paper
56 x 33cm (22 x 13in) piece of floral fabric
Strong (heavy-duty) white thread
Double-sided sticky tape
28 x 75cm (11 x 30in) piece of gingham
Pinking shears
Stranded embroidery thread in yellow, dark green,
*   dark pink, light pink, brown, light green, blue*
*   and violet;*
Small pieces of hessian (burlap)
Iron-on fusible bonding;
2 other floral fabrics
Small red and blue glass beads
Gold lurex thread
25cm (10in) length of narrow ribbon

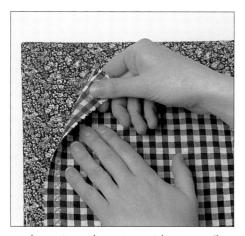

1 Join the two pieces of mounting board along both sides of one long edge with masking tape. Check they can close easily. Cut the water-colour paper to size for the inside pages, fold in half and sew into the spine with strong (heavy-duty) thread. Cover the outside of the book with floral fabric, securing with double-sided tape. Line the inside with gingham. Cut a square of gingham to fit on to the front cover, pink the edges and embroider the border with yellow cross stitch. Stick on to the front of the book with double-sided tape.

2 Cut the hessian (burlap) to fit inside the gingham and fray the edge. Enlarging as necessary, trace the tree, hill and bird from the template on to separate pieces of fusible bonding. Iron on to the back of the floral fabrics and cut out; cut two birds. Remove the backing paper and iron the hill and tree on to the hessian (burlap).

3 Secure the hill and tree with small, dark green stitches. Embroider the leaves in light green by making four small back-stitches and winding the thread around them, or making detached chain stitches. Work lines of brown chain-stitch along the tree trunk and branches.

4 Iron the birds into position. Sew on blue beads for the eyes and stitch the wings in pink, as for leaves. The tail is worked with three detached chain stitches in yellow and blue.

5 Embroider each flower by making a French knot in yellow and surrounding it with five detached chain stitches in blue or violet. Make a stem with a straight stitch in light green and work a leaf. Couch three stars in the sky with gold lurex and sew a few red beads on to the tree as berries.

6 Finish off by working blanket stitch in light pink around the edge of the hessian (burlap) and sticking it on to the front of the book using double-sided tape. Cut the ribbon in half and attach a length to the inside of the front and back covers to make a tie.

Rocket Bag

This small bag uses straight stitch to bold graphic effect, with its futuristic design of space rockets, shooting stars and asteroids. It is worked in a selection of brightly coloured perlé threads on to utilitarian denim. Either side of the background fabric can be used. Each gives a different effect; the steps show the right side and the finished project shows the lighter-coloured reverse.

MATERIALS
Two 2 x 20cm (8in) squares of denim
Dressmaker's chalk or carbon
Embroidery hoop
Perlé cotton embroidery thread in a selection
 of colours
Dressmaker's pins
5 x 25cm (2 x 10in) strip of denim
Pearl button
Blue cotton sewing thread

1 Enlarge the template pattern and transfer the design on to one of the denim pieces, using dressmaker's chalk or carbon. Stretch the fabric in the embroidery hoop and fill in the main shapes of the design with satin stitch.

2 Use the outlines of the design to indicate the stitch direction. Sew parallel lines of simple running stitch to represent the trails left by the flying objects. Refer to the finished picture as a colour guide.

3 With right sides facing, pin and stitch the squares together on three sides. Press under 12mm (½in) around the open edge and hem. For the strap, fold the strip in half lengthways and stitch along the raw edge. Turn through.

4 Slip stitch the strap firmly in place on to the bag. Press the finished bag lightly. Sew the pearl button to the centre front edge of the bag. Make a buttonhole loop on the opposite side using blue cotton sewing thread.

Tea Towel

This cheerful tea towel, with its border of jaunty tea cups, may not stand up to the rigours of drying crockery. It would, however, make a lovely table cover, or would be certain to brighten a small kitchen window if used as a curtain. The cups are cut out of cotton which has been specially coloured with fabric paint and the details are added with back, cross and running stitches.

MATERIALS
Fabric paints and plain cotton fabric or
  scraps of coloured fabric
Tracing paper
Dressmaker's chalk or carbon
Stranded embroidery thread in contrasting colours
Anti-fraying solution or diluted pva adhesive
Striped tea towel

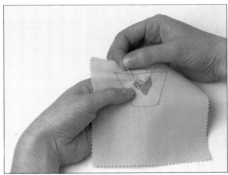

1 The tea cup shapes are cut from cotton fabric. Scraps of coloured cloth would be suitable, or white fabric could be painted specially, using fabric paints. Trace the outlines from the template on to separate pieces of fabric (enlarging to fit), using dressmaker's chalk or carbon.

2 Embroider the pattern details on to the cups with three strands of embroidery thread, using straight or satin stitch. Cut out the cup shapes and tack (baste) them along the border of the tea towel in a pleasing pattern, using the main picture as a guide.

3 If the fabric has been painted, it should not unravel at the edges, but the reverse unpainted side can be coated with a specially manufactured anti-fraying solution or with diluted pva adhesive. Finally, sew the cups in place with back stitch and add extra stitched details.

House and Garden Picture

Gardeners always combined flowers and vegetables in their country plots, and this charming embroidered cottage has a flourishing garden full of both kinds of plants. Basic stitches are imaginatively used to give an added texture to the work. The feathery carrot tops and the cabbages are worked in a loose chain stitch, and the roof is stitched in irregular lines of satin stitch to suggest thatch. The house itself and the windows are outlined in back stitch and the garden is enclosed with a straight stitch picket fence.

MATERIALS

25 x 30cm (10 x 12in) piece of linen fabric
Transfer pencil or water-soluble marker pen
Tracing paper; cotton sewing thread
Stranded embroidery threads in dark and light green,
   pink, orange, red, yellow, rust and dark beige
Anti-fraying solution or diluted pva adhesive
Scraps of cotton fabric in dark and light green, pink,
   orange and red
20 x 25cm (8 x 10in) piece of cardboard
20 x 25cm (8 x 10in) picture frame

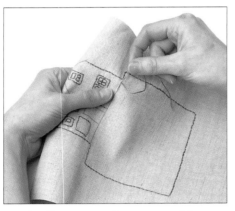

1 Transfer the house and garden outline on to the linen. This can be done by drawing freehand with a water-soluble marker pen, or by tracing the design (enlarged as required) on to tracing paper with a transfer pencil and ironing it on to the fabric. Remember to reverse the design first if using the latter method. Working with three strands of dark beige embroidery thread, back stitch over the outline of the house, garden, door and windows.

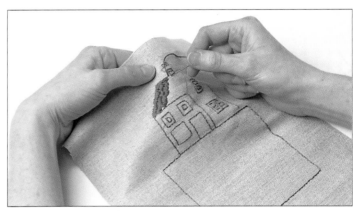

2 Using rust embroidery thread, work the roof and door in satin stitch. The door has three even rows of stitching, while the lines on the roof are less formal and more textured. Next, using dark beige embroidery thread, work a band of satin stitch across the chimney top.

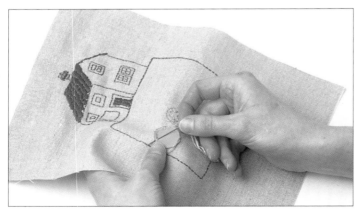

3 Coat the back of the fabric scraps with a proprietary (commercial) anti-fraying solution or with diluted pva adhesive. Cut out four rough circles measuring approximately 2.5cm (1in) in diameter, from light green cotton fabric for the cabbages. Tack (baste) in place, then work the leaf markings in loose chain stitch. Stitch around the outside edge in an uneven blanket stitch.

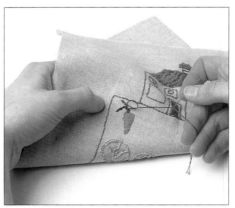

4 Cut sixteen small carrots from orange cotton fabric. Stitch down with running stitch and sew several straight stitches across each shape. The leafy tops are worked in loose chain stitch in dark green. Work the fencing around the border to complete the garden. The flowers, stalks and leaves are cut from cotton fabric and stitched down with running stitch. Embroider a few yellow satin stitches in the centre of the petals. Lightly press the finished work from the back and stretch over the cardboard, lacing firmly at the back with cotton thread, before framing.

Folk Art Gloves

The exuberant floral motif that decorates these gloves was inspired by the patterns on an antique tablecloth from Eastern Europe. The motif has been cleverly adapted to fit on to the back of the hand and along the fingers. The two variations, working on both white and black backgrounds, show how skilful use of colour can alter the appearance of a design. The basic outline is transferred on to the glove as a guide and the embroidery is worked freehand in tapestry wool.

MATERIALS
Pair of white or black woollen gloves
Ruler; pencil; thin cardboard
Tracing paper
Dressmaker's pins
Persian tapestry wool in pink, emerald
  green, royal blue, dark yellow, peach,
  kingfisher blue, bright pink, mint green,
  acid green, lime green and yellow
Tapestry needle

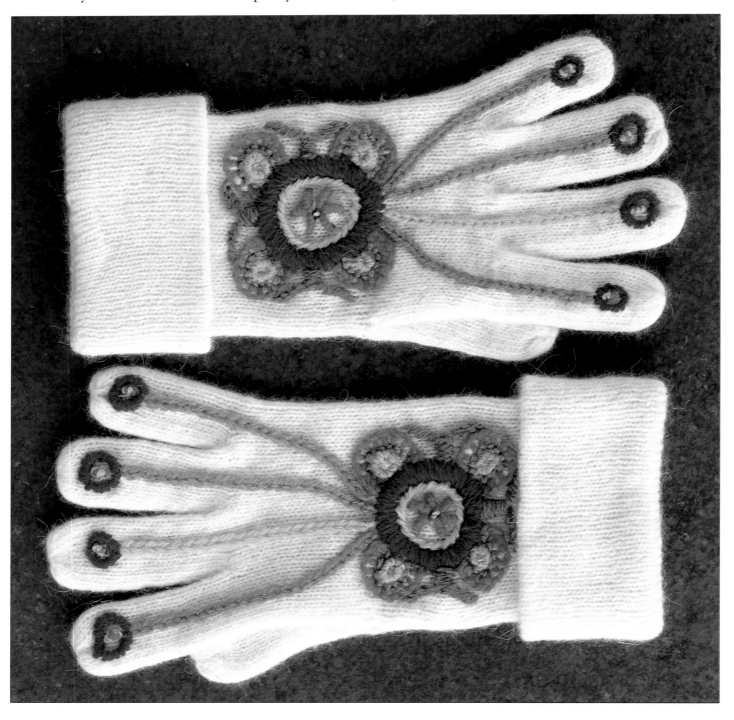

1 To support each glove while embroidering on to it, cut narrow strips from the card to insert in the fingers and a rectangle to fit the palm. Trace the template (enlarging as necessary) and cut out around the outer edge and inner circle. Pin to the glove, matching the top of the template with the finger tips and centring the flower on the back of the hand. Mark the inner circle with a row of small pink running stitches and the dotted lines with emerald green, then remove the template by cutting away between the stitches.

2 Using pink wool, work a circle of satin stitch in the centre of the flower, using the running stitches as a guide. With peach, work a ring of stem stitch close to the inside edge of the centre circle.

3 Embroider the three leaves around the sides and base of the circle in green satin and stem stitch. Unpick the original marker stitches if they still show.

4 Using dark yellow wool, blanket stitch the outer edge of the four petals. Inside this, back stitch a line in royal blue. Fill each with a detached chain stitch, then add a ring of small satin stitches in bright pink wool.

5 Work the stamens in chain stitch, beginning each one between the markers on the centre circle and working down to 2cm (¾in) from the finger tip. Use a different shade of green wool for each one. At the top of each stamen sew a different-coloured circle by making a detached chain stitch and working over it with small satin stitches. In the centre of each circle embroider a striped bullion stitch by threading the needle with one strand each of pink and yellow yarn.

6 Finish the flower by working six bullion stitches in kingfisher blue, arranged in a star pattern to fill the centre circle. To complete, sew a two-coloured bullion stitch in the middle of these stitches.

Hairslide (Barrette)

Decorative hair accessories have always been popular. In the past women needed many pins, combs and clips to keep their elaborate hairstyles in place. These were adorned with everything from feathers, lace and flowers to beads and jewels. This oval hairslide (barrette) is covered with black satin which has been embroidered with flowing lines of silver metallic thread and a contrasting pattern of cream satin stitch. The variation is less formal in design and, with the comb, should provide inspiration for further ideas.

MATERIALS
6.5 x 10cm (2½ x 4in) oval hairslide (barrette)
Tracing paper; tissue paper
Pencil
Remnant of black satin
Embroidery hoop
Cotton sewing thread in black and white
Dressmaker's chalk or carbon; dressmaker's pins
Perlé cotton in black and cream
Silver lurex yarn
Fine silver metallic thread
Remnant of black cotton fabric
Impact adhesive
Iron-on fusible bonding

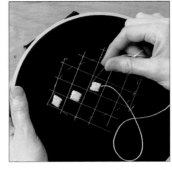

1 Copy the template, adapting it to fit the slide (barrette). Trace the grid and oval outline on to a piece of tissue paper and the oval outline and spirals on to another. Stretch the satin in the hoop and tack (baste) through the tissue with white sewing thread to mark the grid and oval, then remove the paper. Mark the outside edge with chalk 12mm (½in) from the oval outline. Embroider the diamonds alternately in black and cream satin stitch, then take out the tacking.

2 Pin the second piece of tissue paper on to the hoop, lining up the design. Use silver lurex thread for the straight stitch spiral, stitching through the paper. Tear away the tissue and use the same thread to whip over the lines to define them.

3 Use fine silver metallic thread to sew squares on to the black diamonds and black sewing cotton to embroider star stitches on to the cream. Cut out the design around the chalk line.

4 Cut a paper pattern for the backing by drawing round the slide (barrette), marking the position of the clip. Sew a gathering thread around the outside edge of the embroidered fabric and draw up slightly. Place over the slide (barrette) and adjust to fit. Pull the thread tightly, knot the ends and glue down the surplus fabric. Iron the bonding on to the black cotton fabric, then pin the pattern for the backing to this fabric and cut out the backing. Cut a slit in the backing for the clip, then stick the backing on to the slide (barrette).

Drawstring Bag

This sophisticated drawstring bag is embroidered in dark grey, cream and silver threads on two contrasting black background fabrics.

MATERIALS
30 x 90cm (12 x 36in) piece of black satin
30 x 41cm (12 x 16in) piece of black velvet
Black cotton sewing thread; contrasting sewing thread
Embroidery hoop; dressmaker's carbon or chalk
Embroidery thread in dark grey
Silver lurex thread; cream perlé embroidery thread
Fine silver metallic thread; 1.37m (1½ yd) black cord
Safety pin; dressmaker's pins

1 Enlarge the pattern. Cut one piece A from satin and one piece B from velvet for the front. Reverse the templates and repeat for the back. Cut one C from satin and one from velvet. Mark the notches. Stitch the curved edges together to form two rectangles, trim and press the seam. With contrasting thread, tack (baste) from 'a' to 'a' across the centre of each piece to mark the fold line which will eventually be the top of the bag. Work the embroidery on the lower front. Following the main picture, mark three diamonds. Outline with whipped running stitch, with six strands of grey thread.

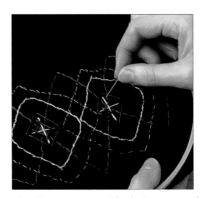

2 Sew the two inner diamonds with silver lurex thread, using whipped running stitch. With cream crochet thread work a second diamond in straight stitch 12mm (½in) outside each of silver shape and stitch a large cross in the centre of each diamond. Outline crosses with dark grey and, with the same thread, stitch a diamond around each (one long stitch per side). With metallic thread work tiny silver crosses between cream straight stitches; couch down the long stitches around crosses. Add final centre crosses with cream perlé thread. Remove from hoop and press.

3 With right sides together, stitch front and back long edges; leave four spaces between notches 'b'. Press seams and top stitch around openings. Pin, tack, then stitch velvet base C to short velvet edges of main piece; right sides together, matching notches. Stitch satin base C to short satin edges of main piece, right sides together. Leave 5cm (2in) gap in seam.

4 Turn bag right sides out through gap. Slipstitch the gap closed. Fold and press along tacked line a-a, and push satin end into velvet end to form a bag with a lining. Stitch lines at 12mm (½in) and 4cm (1½in) down from fold to make a channel for the cord, match with topstitched holes; unpick tacking. Thread cord twice through channel and stitch the two ends together.

Embroidered Hat

The embroidery on the satin brim of this elegant hat uses an interesting selection of textured threads and freestyle stitches. The spiral shapes are worked in whipped running stitch and couching, with sparkling details in metallic thread. The hat itself is made from velvet, and lined with heavy satin to match the turn-back. The coordinating scarf is made from two lengths of velvet with matching embroidery at one end.

MATERIALS
90cm (36 in) burgundy velvet
90cm (36 in) olive-green heavy satin
45cm (18 in) wide green cotton calico
Couching thread; tracing paper; pencil; tissue paper
Matching cotton sewing thread; embroidery hoop
Perlé embroidery thread in crimson and pink
Metallic thread in purple and bronze
Sewing machine; dressmaker's pins

1 Trace the pattern pieces, enlarging as necessary, then cut out in the fabrics indicated, on the bias. Cut a piece of satin 25 x 65cm (10 x 26in) for the embroidered turn-back. Trace the first part of the design on to tissue paper, including the notches in the seam allowance, and tack (baste) through on to the satin. Remove the tissue. Stretch the fabric in a hoop and, starting at the left edge, work the spirals in embroidery thread in a mixture of couched stitches and interlaced double running stitch.

2 Trace off the second part, up to the centre front. Then tack on to the satin, matching notches and marking the centre front notches. Remove the tissue. Embroider the four diamond shapes in straight and satin stitches, and the spirals in a mixture of threads.

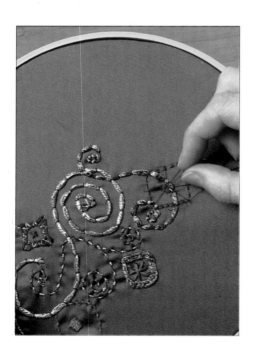

3 Add detail to the diamonds with purple and bronze metallic thread in zigzag stitch or star shapes. Reversing the design, continue along the satin strip, moving it in the hoop, embroidering the right-hand side of the brim with the same stitches and colours as the left.

4 Press the completed embroidery. Pin calico piece C on to the back of the embroidered satin, matching notches. Cut the satin to the same shape as the calico and tack together. Join the centre back seam. Then join centre back seam of velvet piece C, pressing the seams flat. Trim the seam allowance on the velvet. Place the velvet and satin/calico with right sides together and sew along the top edge. Open out, press the seam towards the velvet, and edge-stitch through these layers, close to the seam.

5 Join the centre back seam of velvet piece B (side piece) and press open. Clip along the top edge. With right sides together, pin to velvet piece A (top of hat), matching notches. Tack, then sew together. Repeat with the two satin pieces A and B. Trim the seam allowance on the velvet and press open. Take piece C, turn the velvet over and press on the satin side. Pin together along the lower edge.

6 Pin together the lower edges of velvet pieces B and C, with pile sides together, matching the centre back seams and notches. Turn and sew together 12mm (½in) from the edge. Pin the satin lining in place with the right side facing right side of velvet (as above). Tack, then machine along 12mm (½in) seam allowance, leaving 10cm (4in) space. Pull the hat through this opening, then hand-stitch the space. Finally edge-stitch close to the seam all round to hold the satin lining in place.

Placemat

An ordinary placemat can be changed into a conversation piece for any meal time if it is embroidered with a fanciful trompe-l'oeil place setting. The knives, forks and spoons are worked with several rows of straight stitch in gold thread. This project is a good introduction to using the sewing machine for free stitching, as the firm fabric of the mat does not need to be held within a frame and the outline is easy to follow.

MATERIALS
Ready-made woven placemat
Tissue paper; pencil; dressmaker's pins
Sewing machine
Machine embroidery thread in gold; yellow cotton sewing thread

1 Trace the cutlery designs from the template on to tissue paper, enlarging as necessary. Cut out and arrange the designs on the placemat. Pin in place.

2 Lower the feed dog on the sewing machine and change to a darning foot, using gold thread. Wind the bobbin with yellow sewing thread. Sew a line of straight stitch over the outlines.

3 Having removed the tissue paper, work four closely parallel lines of straight stitch to emphasize the outlines and decoration of the cutlery pieces. Finish off any loose ends.

Cat Picture

Machine embroidery is particularly effective when worked in solid blocks of colour. This sleeping cat is sewn in three varieties of pink, which gives the stitched surface an illusion of light and shade. The background satin stitch has been cut to give a textured tufted finish, which shows to best advantage when the picture is mounted in a deep frame.

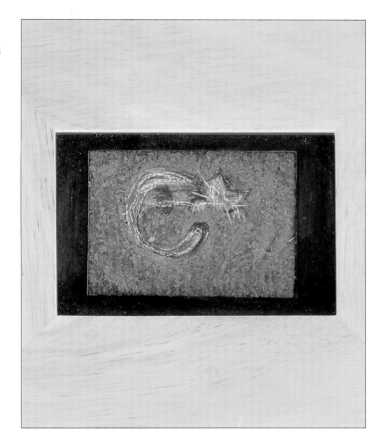

MATERIALS
25cm (10in) square of white cotton fabric
Tracing paper; pencil
Dressmaker's chalk or carbon
Embroidery hoop
Sewing machine
Machine embroidery or sewing thread in 3 shades of
  the main colour and 1 background colour
Embroidery scissors
Contrasting embroidery thread

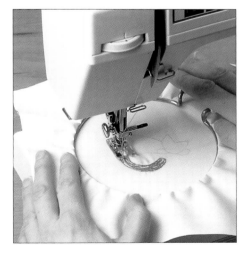

1 Trace the full-size cat outline from the template on to tracing paper. Transfer the design on to the white cotton fabric using dressmaker's chalk or carbon. Stretch the fabric in an embroidery hoop.

2 Lower the feed dog on the sewing machine and, with one shade of the main colour, fill in the outline with straight stitch. Work random lines of the other two shades of the main colour into the stitched surface, marking the paws and back leg.

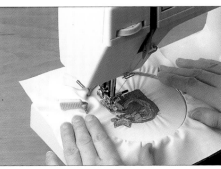

3 Change the top and bottom threads on the machine to the single background colour and adjust the machine to a close zigzag. Slowly work lines of satin stitch to fill in the background, being careful not to stitch over the cat. Remove from the hoop and press lightly.

4 To obtain a textured, carpet-like background to the completed picture, use the sharp point of a pair of embroidery scissors to snip into the solid satin stitch to give a tufted surface. With three strands of contrasting embroidery thread, hand stitch the eyes, whiskers and claws.

Picture Frame

The paintings of Gustav Klimt, the Austrian symbolist artist, were the influence behind this decorative photograph frame. The jewel-like surfaces of his work are densely patterned with geometric shapes and sinuous lines, reminiscent of brocades, silks and other luxurious textiles. The embroidery is machine-worked in a free straight-stitch with a darning foot, and the fabric feed is lowered to allow a greater fluidity of movement.

MATERIALS

20 x 25cm (8 x 10in) piece of black velvet
20 x 25cm (8 x 10in) piece of metallic organza
Tissue paper; pencil; embroidery hoop
2 pieces of 15 x 20cm (6 x 8in) mounting (mat) board
Sewing machine
Machine embroidery thread in gold, cream, yellow and light blue
20 x 25cm (8 x 10in) piece of self-adhesive black felt
Black cotton sewing thread; pva adhesive
Short length of cord for the hanging loop

1 Trace the design from the template on to tissue paper, enlarging as required. Layer the tissue, organza and velvet and tack together across the centre and then around the edges. Stretch the fabric in a hoop.

2 Thread the machine with gold thread and use a darning foot. Lower the feed dog and set to straight stitch, then sew along the wavy lines and around the triangles, moving the frame as necessary.

3 Tear off the tissue paper and fill in the triangles with rows of straight stitch, using the various coloured threads. Thread all the loose ends of cotton to the back of the work.

4 Cut a rectangle from the centre of one of the pieces of mounting (mat) cardboard, to leave a 3.5cm (1½in) wide frame. Place on the reverse of the embroidery and cut out the middle section, leaving a 12mm (½in) seam allowance.

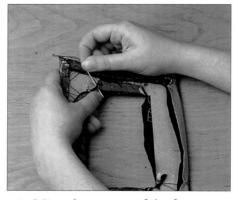

5 Mitre the corners of the frame, then fold the edges to the back and pull together with large stitches, making sure that the corners are tidy Take the second piece of board and cover with self-adhesive felt.

6 Glue the board to the frame along the two sides and bottom edge, so that the picture can be inserted from the top. Attach a short length of cord to the back of the frame to make a hanging loop, or make a simple stand from a triangle of cardboard which has been covered with black felt.

Fish Mobile

Shimmering gauzes and translucent organzas (organdy) give a wonderfully watery feel to this mobile, which would look equally at home in the bathroom or the nursery. The seahorses, fish and seaweed are worked in metallic machine embroidery threads on to water-soluble fabric. This special technique means that fine, net-like fabrics can be created, which are ideally suited to the seaside theme.

MATERIALS
Water-soluble fabric; indelible felt-tip pen; tracing paper; pen; embroidery hoop; sewing machine
Assortment of crystalline and metallic organzas (organdies), tinsel and other shiny fabrics; dressmaker's pins
Matching metallic machine embroidery threads
60cm (24in) length of 12mm (½ in) dowelling
Blue and green diluted craft paints
Nylon fishing line; clear glass beads

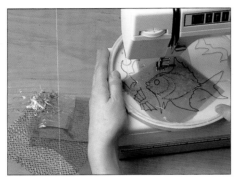

1 Copy the templates for the fish, seaweed and seahorse, enlarging as necessary. Trace a fish and a frond of seaweed on to water-soluble fabric and put into the hoop. Cut two scraps of organza and sandwich small fragments of metallic fabrics between them for the body. Pin to the underside of hoop. Thread machine with metallic thread, lower feed dog and set to straight stitch. Sew around the main body and head.

2 Work the seaweed in the same way as step 1, using matching green thread and green organza. Extra freedom in stitching can be achieved by removing the presser foot on the sewing machine, but this way of working demands special care in handling the hoop, and is not absolutely necessary.

3 Turn the embroidery hoop over and trim back the excess fabric, then, to complete the fish, work the main fins and tail by outlining them with a zigzag stitch, filling in the space with interlacing lines of straight stitch. Work the two separate fins in the same way, then work a frilly zigzag stitch around the seaweed.

4 Dip the completed pieces of the mobile into water and allow the water-soluble backing fabric to dissolve. Rinse the pieces carefully to remove any traces of the backing fabric, then dry each on a towel, away from direct heat.

5 Following the same method, make eight extra lengths of seaweed, two seahorses and four more fish. Alter the shape and colour schemes so that the fish are all different. Attach each fish to a piece of fishing line, varying the lengths. Twist seaweed around the line and sew in place.

6 Cut the dowel into one 25cm (10in) and two 18cm (7in) lengths and stain with the craft paint. Stitch the seaweed to the dowel as shown. Hang the mobile and adjust so that it is evenly balanced. Sew glass beads to the fish and seaweed, to add both extra weight and decoration.

Table Cloth

Water-soluble fabric can be adapted to a variety of uses when embroidering with the sewing machine. It is usually used as a foundation for making net-like fabrics, but it also serves as an effective support when two materials of very different weights are being used. For this project, delicate openwork motifs in pearly white organza (organdy) are set into a heavy linen table cloth to make an attractive centrepiece.

MATERIALS
Dressmaker's chalk or carbon
Linen table cloth
Tissue paper
30 x 60cm (12 x 24in) piece of white organza (organdy)
30 x 60cm (12 x 24in) piece of water-soluble fabric
Dressmaker's pins
White cotton sewing thread; sewing machine
Embroidery hoop; sharp embroidery scissors

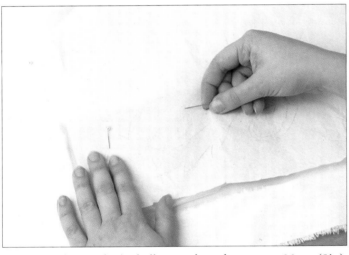

1 With dressmaker's chalk or carbon draw out a 20cm (8in) square centrally on the reverse side of the table cloth. Trace the cut-out design on to tissue paper and use the main picture as a guide to setting out the motifs. Cut a piece of organza (organdy) and water-soluble fabric to size and line up along one side of the square. Pin the tissue paper on top.

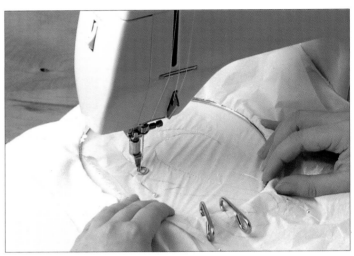

2 Thread the machine with white thread, lower the feed dog and put on a darning foot. Place the fabric in an embroidery hoop. Following the marked line, straight stitch around the motif, then remove the tissue paper.

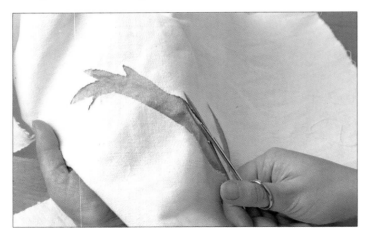

3 Turn the cloth over and, with sharp scissors, cut away the linen from inside the shape, taking care not to snip through either the outline stitches or the organza.

4 Set the machine to a wide close satin stitch and sew over the straight stitch line enclosing the raw edges. Work the other four sides of the square in the same way, then wash away the water-soluble fabric in cold water. Allow to dry, then press.

Needlepoint

Needlepoint involves working stitches on to a canvas to create geometric or illustrative designs. Its simplicity means that it is growing in popularity, and only a needle, some yarn and a piece of canvas are required to get started. Many ready-to-work kits are available, but, with some knowledge, it is easy to create individual pieces, from simple tent stitch pictures to elaborate textured cushions (pillows).

Jewellery Box

The soft, natural earth colours of this jewellery box echo the subtle, faded shades which are typical of old textiles. A simple outline for the pattern itself is given here, however, the actual yarns used can be chosen almost at random, and then blended together for an informal effect. The plastic canvas used for the lid is ideal for constructing three-dimensional objects; it is simple to cut to any size and strong enough to hold its shape.

MATERIALS
12.5 x 20cm (5 x 8in) piece of plastic canvas
Waterproof felt-tip pen
Tapestry yarn in a selection of toning colours
Tapestry needle
36 x 90cm (14 x 36in) piece of self-adhesive black felt
30cm (12in) square of sturdy cardboard
Metal ruler
Cutting board
Craft knife

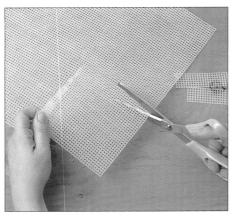

1 Cut the box lid sections from the plastic canvas: one 12.5cm (5in) square, and four 2 x 12.5cm (¾ x 5in) rectangles to form the sides. Enlarge then trace the template on to the canvas with a waterproof pen. Work the design in tent stitch, blending the colours using two toning strands.

2 Sew the four side pieces of the fold in the same way as step 1, then overstitch the long edges to the square using two different colours of yarn in the needle. Join the short edges to complete the lid.

3 Overstitch the raw edges of the canvas to make a neat border. Cut an 18cm (7in) square of self-adhesive black felt to line the box lid. Clipping the corners to fit, peel off the backing paper and stick in place, trimming the lower edge as necessary.

4 To make the main box, mark a 11.5cm (4½in) square in the centre of the cardboard. Then on each side rule a 9 x 11.5cm (3½ x 4½in) rectangle. Cut out the cross shape and score along the folds.

5 Using this shape as a guide, cut out two pieces of black felt for the inside and outside of the box, each with tabs on the four sides and 12mm(½in) turn-over around the top edge on one piece.

6 Fold the cardboard along the scored lines and cover the outside with the felt, using the tabs to secure the corners and folding over at the top. Use the second piece of felt to line the inside of the box.

Lone-Star Cushion (Pillow)

This needlepoint cushion (pillow)is an adaptation of an Amish patchwork bedcover design from the 1930s and reflects their mastery of colour. Its strong graphic impact relies upon the interaction of light and dark shades in muted tones, which radiate from the centre in concentric rings. The design is worked in a diagonal stitch, which gives it an almost padded effect, suggesting the quilted patterns of the original cover.

MATERIALS

41cm (16in) square of 12-count single-thread canvas
Masking tape; tapestry needle; cotton sewing thread
Tapestry frame (optional)
Tapestry yarn:
  1 skein each in pale lilac, dark peach, indigo, orange, crimson and dark gold
  2 skeins in light turquoise
  6 skeins in dark turquoise
  6 skeins in dark purple
Matching velvet or needlecord fabric for the backing
30cm (12in) cushion (pillow) pad

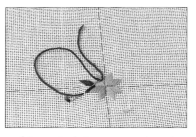

1 Bind the edges of the canvas with masking tape to prevent them unravelling. Find the middle of the canvas by folding it in half each way and sew two rows of tacking stitch in contrasting thread to divide it into quarters. Mount the canvas on a frame if desired. Using the tacking lines as a guide, stitch the centre star in pale lilac yarn, working diagonally over four threads of canvas. Following the chart, sew the next round in dark purple.

2 Work the next four rounds in dark peach, indigo, dark turquoise, then light turquoise, and then continue with the dark purple round that starts to divide the points of the star, carrying the thread behind the work.

3 Using the picture as a guide, work the points, starting and finishing each colour separately. Fill the dark turquoise background in diagonal stitch.

4 Work a border of three lines of dark purple diagonal stitch, in the direction of the previous stitches. Stretch and block the work into shape, then cut a 33cm (13in) square of backing fabric. With right sides together, join to the canvas on three sides, turn right way out, insert the cushion (pillow) pad and slip stitch the final side closed.

Nine-Star Cushion (Pillow)

The nine-star is a variation of the distinctive lone-star quilt design. The basic unit is an eight-pointed star, which is repeated in three rows of three, to produce an interesting secondary pattern of squares and diamonds. The stars are worked in complementary faded tones of burgundy, rust and pinks, in diagonal stitch, and the cream background in textured cushion (pillow) stitch.

MATERIALS

41cm (16in) square of 12-count single-thread canvas
Masking tape; cotton sewing thread; tapestry needle
Tapestry frame (optional)
Tapestry yarn:
  8 skeins in cream
  1 skein each in pale lemon and light gold
  2 skeins each in pale pink, rust and burgundy
  3 skeins each in dark pink and dark gold
Toning fabric for the backing
30cm (12in) cushion (pillow) pad

1 Bind the outside edge of the canvas with masking tape to prevent it fraying. Mark the middle of the canvas with two lines of running stitch in contrasting thread, then mount on a frame if desired. Use the guides to position the centre star. Following the chart, work the first round with pale lemon yarn, using a diagonal stitch over three threads of canvas. Work the next two rounds in light gold and pale pink.

2 Stitch the next round in dark pink, then work the tapering diamond points following the main photograph. Find the position of the four stars around the centre star by stitching the diamonds at their tips, where they touch the outer points of the first star.

3 Work the four corner stars in the same way. Fill in the background with cushion (pillow) stitch squares using cream yarn. Work the other eight diamonds, then stitch a final row of cushion (pillow) stitch around the edge. Stretch and block the finished piece. Cut the backing fabric to the same size and sew together round three edges, with right sides facing. Turn the right way out, insert the cushion (pillow) pad and slip stitch the fourth side closed.

Heart Picture

The heart is the ultimate symbol of love and affection, and as such recurs throughout the applied arts of many cultures. For this dramatic tent stitch panel, one basic motif is repeated six times, in a format influenced by the Pop Art screen prints of Andy Warhol. The vibrant colour comes from blending individual strands of Persian yarn, which is dyed in particularly intense hues.

1 Plan the colour combinations before starting to sew. Choose complementary shades for subtle backgrounds, such as the pale blue and lilac square, and contrasting tones – lime and emerald green – for more impact.

2 Separate the yarn into strands and, working with two strands at a time, work the heart motifs in tent stitch. Follow the chart, on which one square represents one stitch.

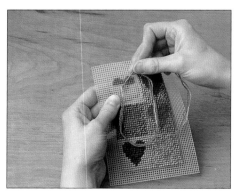

3 Vary the colour within some individual shapes; two different pinks are used for the final heart. Plastic canvas has the great advantage that it does not need to be blocked into shape, so it is suited to work that will be framed. Trim the finished piece to fit the frame using sharp scissors.

MATERIALS
Persian yarn in a selection of pinks, reds, blues and greens
Tapestry needle
11.5 x 15cm (4½ x 6in) piece of 10-count plastic canvas
7.5 x 11.5cm (3 x 4½in) picture frame
Embroidery scissors

Circular Star

Plastic canvas is available in round shapes of various sizes, as well as in the more usual square grid pattern. This gives great scope for experimentation with designs based on the geometric division of a circle. Stars and snowflake motifs naturally lend themselves to this, and make unusual Christmas decorations. The scale of this project makes it a good way to use up small amounts of yarn. Use the photograph as a stitching guide.

MATERIALS
7.5cm (3in) diameter plastic canvas disc
Waterproof felt-tip pen (optional)
Tapestry needle
Tapestry wool yarn in a selection of toning colours
Small piece of self-adhesive felt
30cm (12in) length of satin ribbon

1 Copy the star design from the template. (The pattern could be traced directly on to the canvas with a waterproof felt-tip pen.) Thread the needle with two different coloured yarns to create a mottled effect. Stitch one-quarter of the design at a time, working from the centre outwards. To secure the ends of the yarn do not knot them, but leave a length and catch under the back when stitching.

2 Using the main picture as a guide to colour, finish off the outside edge by slip stitching.

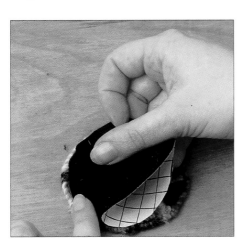

3 Cut a 7.5cm (3in) circle of self-adhesive felt. Peel off the protective paper and stick the felt to the back of the work so that it conceals the ends.

4 Fold the ribbon in half and stitch to the edge of the disc. Knot the ends together and trim.

Cup and Saucer

The familiar domestic image of a floral china tea cup and saucer is captured in this needlepoint design. The main part is worked in tent stitch with a border of cushion (pillow) stitch squares. The background is stitched in two shades of the same colour, graded from dark to light. The distinctive shape of the frame – known as an Oxford frame – gives the finished picture a rural aspect and charm.

MATERIALS

20 x 25cm (8 x 10in) piece of 12-count single-thread canvas
Waterproof felt-tip pen
Tapestry needle
1 skein Persian yarn each in dark and light olive, dark and light rust, dark and light pink, light gold, turquoise, dark blue and cream

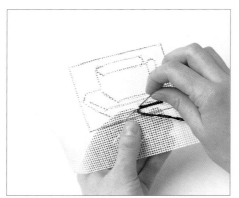

1 Trace the cup and saucer template directly on to the canvas, using a waterproof felt-tip pen with a fine point. Work the main outline in dark blue tent stitch. Stitch a line of turquoise as a drop shadow.

2 Work the border around the rim and the flowers in pink, the leaves in olive and turquoise, the flower centres in gold and the cup in cream. With two shades of rust, fill in the background rectangle in tent stitch.

3 Next, work three rounds of cushion (pillow) stitch over four threads as a border, using olive for the final round. Stretch and block the finished piece, then fold under the surplus canvas and press.

Sun Pincushion

The sunburst is a universal image of life and energy. Like the heart, it appears as a decorative motif in various forms throughout the world. This interpretation is based on a drawing from a Renaissance manuscript and is worked in three rich golden shades of Persian yarn, with a contrasting cobalt blue background. Basic tent stitch is used throughout, and the finished design is framed with three bands of long-arm cross stitch.

MATERIALS
20cm (8in) square of 10-count double-thread canvas
Masking tape; tacking (basting) thread
Waterproof felt-tip pen; tapestry needle
1 skein Persian yarn each in pale yellow, dark golden
  yellow, warm gold, mid blue, chocolate brown
  and white
Matching cotton sewing thread
41 x 90cm (16 x 36in) piece of polyester wadding
  (batting)
Dressmaker's pins; matching fabric for the backing

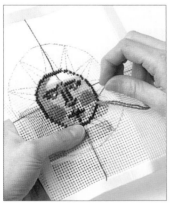

1 Bind the edges of the canvas with masking tape to prevent them fraying and mark the centre with two lines of tacking stitch. Trace the design or draw it directly on to the canvas. Use two strands of yarn in the needle throughout. Outline the face first in brown, then pick out the cheeks, eyes, nose and mouth details using the photograph as a guide to colours.

2 Fill in the circle surrounding the face in blue, with rays of pale yellow and warm gold, then complete the square in white. Next, stitch three lines of long-arm cross stitch, using progressive shades of pale yellow, dark golden yellow, then warm gold, to frame the sun. Stretch and block the finished work.

3 Make a pad to fill the cushion (pillow): cut two 15cm (6in), four 12.5cm (5in) and three 10cm (4in) squares of wadding (batting) and stack them as shown. Pin, then stitch together.

4 Cut an 18cm (7in) square of backing fabric and, right sides together, pin and stitch to the needlepoint on three sides. Turn under the 12mm (½in) seam allowance on the fourth side, insert the pad and slip stitch the side closed.

Brooch Cushion (Pillow)

A brooch cushion (pillow) can look very attractive, set among ornaments and cosmetic jars on the dressing table, and it is a good way to display a selection of favourite jewellery. The toning blues of this frilled version have been picked to match the fabric ruffle, but the colour scheme could easily be adapted to coordinate with the furnishings of a particular room.

MATERIALS
25cm (10in) square of 12-count single-thread canvas
Masking tape; tacking (basting) thread
Tapestry yarn:
 2 skeins each in white, pale blue and mid blue
 1 skein each in dark blue and indigo
50 x 75cm (20 x 30in) piece of polyester wadding
 (batting); tapestry needle; dressmaker's pins;
matching cotton sewing thread
20cm (8in) square of printed fabric for the backing
 20 x 122cm (4 x 48in) printed
 fabric for the frill
 Sewing machine

44

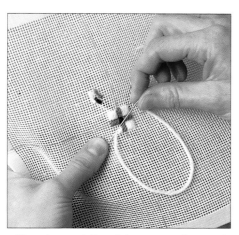

1 Bind the edges of the canvas with masking tape and mark the centre with two lines of contrasting tacking stitch. The checked pattern is worked in diagonal stitch throughout. Start off in the middle of the canvas by working a small square over two threads, using indigo wool. Work a narrow line of mid blue on each side of the square and fill in the corners with white squares.

2 Following the chart, continue to work the checked pattern until the stitched area measures 14.5cm (5¾in). All the stitches should be worked so that they face the same direction, which will mean that the finished piece becomes distorted. Stretch and block it back into a square shape.

3 Make a cushion (pillow) pad by cutting four 16.5cm (6½in), four 14cm (5½in) and four 11.5cm (4in) squares of wadding (batting) and sandwiching them together as shown. Pin around the edge, sew, then trim away the excess. Cut a 16.5cm (6½in) square of backing fabric and, with right sides together, sew to the needlepoint around three sides, sewing close to the stitches. Turn through, clip the corners and press. Insert the cushion (pillow) pad and slip stitch the fourth side closed.

4 Join the short edges of the frill with a French seam, then make a narrow hem all around each long side, turning the fabric over twice to conceal the raw edges.

5 Run a strong gathering thread around one side. Fold the frill into four to mark it into quarters, then pin around the four sides of the cushion (pillow).

6 Draw up the thread and adjust the gathers so that they are even, allowing an extra fullness at the corners. Stitch on to the cushion (pillow) using small neat stitches, and working from the right side.

Needle Book and Scissor Case

A holder for needles is essential for everybody who sews, and this ivy-leaf needle book, with its matching scissor case, would make an appropriate gift for an embroiderer. Both are trimmed with cord, and the scissor case has a long loop so that it can be kept within easy reach when working. The symmetrical shape of the dark green leaves is offset by the trailing coils of couched gold thread. The informality of this naturalistic design means that there is no need to be too rigid in placing the leaves or copying the stem lines.

NEEDLE BOOK MATERIALS
Ruler; waterproof felt-tip pen
20 x 25cm (8 x 10in) piece of 12-count single thread
  canvas; tapestry needle
Gold metallic thread for the stems
1 skein of tapestry yarn in dark green and 6 skeins in
  light green; matching cotton sewing thread
12.5 x 18cm (5 x 7in) piece of green lining fabric
25cm (10in) square of felt; 70cm (28in) length of cord

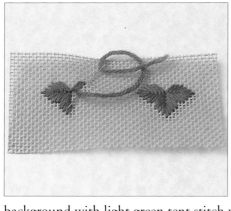

1 Using a waterproof felt-tip pen, rule a rectangle of 10 x 15cm (4 x 6in) on to the canvas. Trace the design. Stitch the leaves in dark green straight stitch. Fill in the background with light green tent stitch worked on the diagonal from the top right-hand corner. Couch a double strand of gold thread for the stems and tendrils.

2 Press the finished piece lightly, then cut out, adding 12mm (½in) canvas all round. Finger-press turnings to the wrong side. Cut the lining to the same size as the canvas. Press under the 12mm (½in) seam allowance, mitring the corners. Slip stitch to the back of the canvas and press from the wrong side on to a padded surface.

3 Cut four felt pages, slightly smaller than half the finished cover size, and stitch to the back cover.

4 Slip stitch cord around the outer edge of the cover, starting and finishing at the centre top. Knot the ends into a loop.

1 Following the diagram, draw the case outline on to the canvas. Work the four leaves in dark green straight stitch. Fill in the background in tent stitch in light green and couch a double strand of gold thread for the stems and tendrils. Make two pieces, reversing the design for the back.

SCISSOR CASE MATERIALS
Waterproof felt-tip pen
20 x 25cm (8 x10in) piece of 12-count single-thread canvas; tapestry needle
1 skein of tapestry yarn in dark green and 5 skeins in light green
Gold metallic thread for the stems
15 x 20cm (6 x 8in) piece of lining fabric
Sewing machine; matching cotton sewing thread; length of cord

2 Cut out one piece, leaving a margin around the stitching, and cut a piece of lining to the same size. With right sides of canvas and lining facing, stitch close to the worked area down one long side and up the other, leaving the top unstitched between points A and A.

3 Trim the surplus fabric around the stitched line as shown and clip the angles. Clip the canvas and trim the lining on the unstitched top edge. Press under the excess on both sides.

4 Gently turn through to the right side, making sure that the corners are crisp. Tidy the turn-in around the top edge and stitch the lining and canvas together. Lay the work face downwards on a soft pad and press. Repeat the lining process for the second side.

5 With the wrong sides together, slip stitch the two sides, leaving the top open between points A. Trim with cord. Attach the cord to one point A, 35cm (14in) from one end. Slip stitch all around the top opening, then down one side and up the other. Join securely at second point A and cut the two long ends to equal lengths. Tie the two ends together in a knot.

Patchwork and Quilting

To create patchwork, small pieces of fabric are sewn together to make items that can range in scale from a tiny pincushion to a bedcover. The joy of this process is that, even when using a traditional pattern and scraps of recycled cloth, each project will be unique. The beauty of each design lies in its combination of shapes and colours; with imagination, almost anything is possible.

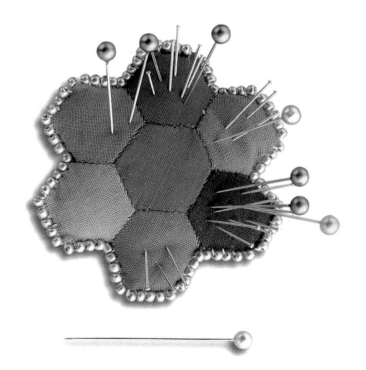

Checked Cushion (Pillow)

This checked cushion (pillow) is a unique mixture of the old and new. The green and red gingham cloth has been taken from outworn garments, while the antique engravings have been transferred on to cotton material, using a newly developed technique. Image transfer is an exciting medium, by which any photocopied picture can be fixed on to fabric, and its possibilities are endless.

MATERIALS
Image-transfer (photo transfer) solution
Illustrations of fruit and vegetables
Scraps of checked and gingham fabric
White cotton fabric
Cushion (pillow) pad
Sewing thread; decorative buttons

3 Sew the patches together, starting with the shortest edges first and pressing all the seams open. Sew on the buttons for a decorative finish. Cut a piece of fabric 12mm (½in) larger all round than the cushion pad and, with right sides facing, pin to the patchwork piece. Sew together around three sides and clip the corners. Turn through and press lightly, then insert the cushion (pillow) pad and slip stitch the fourth side closed.

1 Photocopy your chosen engravings, enlarging the scale if necessary, and cut out. Use special image-copying solution to transfer the photocopies on to plain white cotton fabric, following the manufacturer's instructions.

2 Collect together a selection of toning checked fabrics and scraps, and cut them into rectangular shapes. Cut the transferred images to size and sort the various patches into a pleasing arrangement that fits the size of the cushion (pillow) pad.

Red Star

The bold combination of turkey red and plain white was a favourite colour scheme among nineteenth-century American quilters. This project continues the thrifty tradition of early patchwork, using re-cycled cotton sheeting which has been dyed in two different shades of dark red. The variation in colour adds a dynamic quality to the surface of the quilt. It is worked in the English style, using backing papers, but the patches could equally be sewn together by machine. The finished piece measures 70cm (28in) square.

MATERIALS
Old white cotton bed sheet
Hot-water dye in scarlet and crimson
Thick paper for cutting the templates
Tracing paper
Tacking thread
Cotton sewing thread
Beeswax; dressmaker's pins
75cm (30in) square of iron-on quilting

1 Discard any worn areas of the sheet. Following the manufacturer's instructions, dye half of the fabric in two shades of red. Trace the inner diamond template accurately and use it to cut out 72 backing papers. From the cotton cut 40 red and 32 white diamonds, using the outer template as a guide. Tack a fabric diamond to each paper one, folding over the surplus fabric at the points.

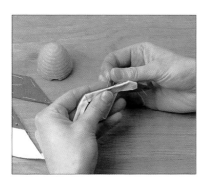

2 Overstitch the edges of the diamonds together with right sides facing. Pull the sewing thread over a block of beeswax to prevent it fraying. Assemble eight large diamonds, following the finished picture.

3 Join the eight diamonds together to form a star, making sure that the centre points all butt together tidily. Press from the right side, then remove the papers.

4 Cut a 54cm (21in) square of white cotton. From red cotton, cut four 12.5 x 54cm (5 x 21in) strips and four 12.5cm (5in) squares. Sew two of the strips to opposite sides of the main square, leaving a 12mm (½in) seam allowance. Join a red square to each end of the other two strips and sew in place to complete the border. Pin the star to the centre of the white square.

5 Slip stitch the star in place, tucking under any surplus fabric. Cut the iron-on quilting into a square measuring 12mm (½in) less than the panel and fix to the reverse side. Back with cotton and tidy up the edges.

Saw-Tooth Star Bag

The saw-tooth star pattern, like many other patchwork patterns, derives its name from the simple surroundings of everyday life: the triangular shapes around the four sides suggest the sharp teeth of a saw blade. The star, an old variation of the basic four-square block, is ideally suited to the homespun cotton checks which make this useful drawstring bag.

MATERIALS
Tracing paper
Pencil
Remnants of 3 different checked fabrics
Matching cotton sewing thread
Safety pin
Dressmaker's pins
Potpourri or lavender flowers

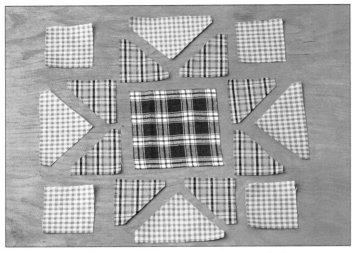

1 Enlarge and trace the templates, which include a seam allowance. Cut one large square from the darkest fabric, four small squares and four large triangles from the mid-tone, and eight small triangles from the lightest check.

2 Join the small and large triangles together, piecing by hand or machine. Press the seam allowance to one side, away from the large triangle. Pin one block to each of two opposite sides of the main square, then stitch. Press the seams outwards.

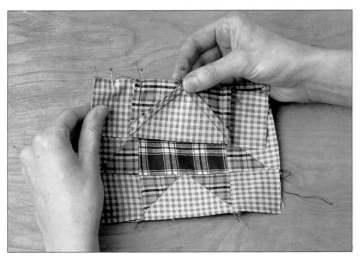

3 Take the small squares of mid-tone fabric and join one to each end of the other two blocks. Pin these to the main piece, along the long edges. Stitch the seams, then press so that they lie facing away from the centre square.

4 Cut two rectangles of 16.5 x 27cm (6½ x 10½in) and 16.5 x 42cm (6½ x 16½in) from the mid-tone fabric. Sew the smaller piece to one side of the square, and the longer piece to the opposite edge, allowing for a 6mm (¼in) seam. Fold in half, right sides together, and join the side seams. Turn through, fold top in half, turn in and hem.

5 Sew a 2.5cm (1in) wide drawstring channel, 2.5cm (1in) down from the top edge. Take out the side seam between the two rows of stitching on the right-hand side. Cut a length of matching fabric measuring 5 x 60cm (2 x 24in). Sew it together lengthways, 12mm (½in) away from the raw edges.

6 Trim the seam allowance on the matching fabric and fasten a safety pin to one end. Feed this back inside the tube and turn the drawstring through. Press, then thread through the channel, tying the ends in a knot. Fill the bag with potpourri or lavender flowers.

Log-Cabin Yarn Roll

A full-sized cover in log-cabin patchwork would provide a colourful and dramatic focal point in any bedroom. Undertaking a large-scale quilt, however, is a real labour of love which can take many months, if not years. This yarn holder, which is made from three log-cabin blocks, is a perfect compromise for those whose time is limited. It is a good way to learn how the design is assembled and how its visual impact relies on the contrast between light and dark fabrics.

MATERIALS

Fabric marker pen; dressmaker's pins
20 x 56cm (8 x 22in) piece of calico or other cotton fabric
Selection of cotton fabric pieces sorted into dark and light patterns
20 x 51cm (8 x 20in) piece of patterned fabric for the lining
Sewing machine; matching cotton sewing thread
1.37m (1½yd) length of 12mm (½in) ribbon

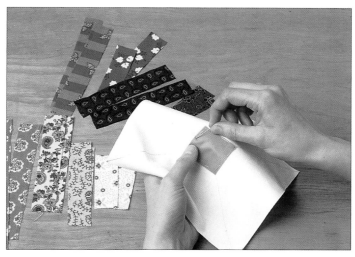

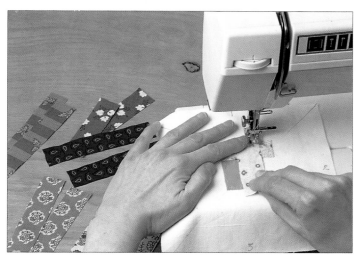

1 For each of the three blocks, cut an 18cm (7in) square from plain fabric. Draw two diagonal lines across the square to mark the centre and to help position the strips. Cut a 4.5cm (1¾in) square of plain-coloured fabric and tack (baste) to the centre of the square. Cut 3cm (1¼in) strips of fabric for the four rounds that will surround the square, using the template as a guide, enlarging if necessary.

2 Place the first light strip, pattern side down, along the top edge of the central square. Lower the feed dog on the machine and stitch down along the outside edge. Fold back and press flat. Working clockwise, sew on the second light strip in the same way, then the two dark strips.

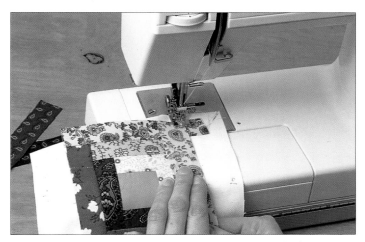

3 Continue stitching the strips down in rounds, keeping the dark and light colours on opposite sides, and overlapping each round to allow a 6mm (¼in) seam.

4 Sew the three blocks together in a row and press the seams open. Cut a rectangle of lining fabric which is the same width as, and slightly longer than, the strip. With right sides together, pin and sew along the two long sides and one short end, clip the corners, turn through and press. Fold the overlapping end tidily over the patchwork, pin and slip stitch down.

5 Sew a length of ribbon to the outside of the roll to form a tie.

Crazy Quilt

The random patterning of crazy patchwork makes it quick and enjoyable to work; it does not require a great deal of pre-planning or accurate measurement. This small quilt – which would make a good play mat for a baby – is made from an assortment of striped cotton fabrics. The raw edges are concealed with lines of dark red feather-stitching, which contrasts with the pastel blues and pinks of the shirting. The finished quilt measures 60cm (24in) square.

MATERIALS
Scraps of striped cotton shirting and chambray
Dressmaker's pins
Cotton sewing thread
Stranded embroidery thread in dark red
70cm (28in) square of lightweight iron-on wadding (batting)
70cm (28in) square of backing fabric

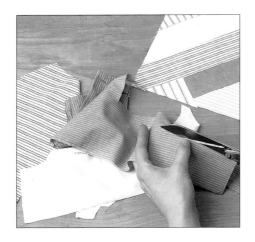

1 Cut a 20cm (8in) square of plain fabric. From the striped cottons cut out irregular strips and shapes, then lay them out on the foundation square, in an interesting pattern.

2 Pin the pattern in place and sew down with running stitch. Sew the outer edges, then with three strands of dark red thread, work lines of feather stitching over the joins.

3 Make a further eight blocks, then join them in three rows of three. Sew the three strips together and press the seams open.

4 Cut the iron-on wadding (batting) to the same size as the patchwork and, following the manufacturer's instructions, iron it on to the reverse side.

5 From the backing fabric cut a square that measures 5cm (2in) greater than the quilt. Press under 12mm (½in) all round, then pin to the back of the quilt. Fold the tidied edge over to the right side and slip stitch securely down, mitring the corners.

Linen Throw

In the past, the care of domestic linen – pillow cases, sheets, napkins, table cloths and runners – was an essential part of household management, and in the wealthiest homes special maids were employed to look after the laundry. Many mats, cloths and covers have survived, but they are not always practical for ordinary use. This all-white quilt is made up of squares cut from old linen, and uses the most interesting types of insertion, embroidery, monograms and pintucking.

MATERIALS
Assortment of old household textiles
Fabric marker pen (washable)
Thin cardboard; dressmaker's pins
White cotton sewing thread
Traditional cotton batting or polyester wadding
Old bed sheet
Contrasting cotton sewing thread
Thick white crochet cotton
Large-eyed sharp needle

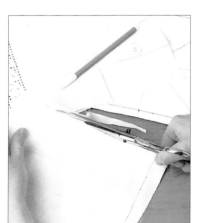

1 The quilt can be made to any size, depending on the amount of fabric available. Cut a 20cm (8in) square from thin cardboard to use as a template. Selecting the best textures and patterns, draw around the template on to the fabric and cut a series of patches.

2 Spread the squares out and arrange in regular rows. Using white cotton, sew in pairs, pressing the seams open. Then join into blocks of four and sew the blocks together until the whole quilt top has been pieced together.

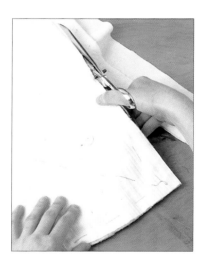

3 Cut a piece of batting or wadding the same size as the patchwork, joining if necessary. Use an old bed sheet to back the work, and tack (baste) three layers together with a contrasting thread. Trim back the wadding and the backing layer so that they measure 2cm (¾in) less than the quilt.

4 Thread a large-eyed needle with crochet cotton and back stitch through all three layers at one-corner intersection. Tie the ends tightly with a reef or weaver's knot and trim to 12mm (½in). Repeat over the whole surface.

5 Turn under a 12mm (½in) hem all around the quilt top and fold the surplus over to the wrong side. Slip stitch to the backing fabric, mitring the corners.

Chair Seat

Two different colourways of the same floral furnishing chintz are used for this padded chair seat, giving a chequerboard (checkerboard) effect. "Tied quilting", using narrow pink ribbon, holds the layers together, and ribbon bows are used to attach the pad to the chair. The project serves as an introduction to cutting and piecing basic square patches, and shows how to match the seams together for a professional result.

MATERIALS
Rotary cutter; cutting board
Quilter's square
Remnants of floral furnishing fabric
Dressmaker's pins; matching cotton sewing thread
90cm (36in) length of 2.5cm (1in) ribbon
90cm (36in) length of 10mm (⅜in) ribbon
Thick polyester wadding (batting)
Large-eyed sharp needle

1 With the quilter's square and a rotary cutter, cut out eight light and eight dark squares from the floral fabric, each measuring 10cm (4in). Hold the cutter upright on the cutting board, and always move it away from the body, as the blade is very sharp.

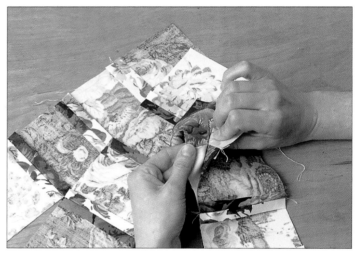

2 Lay the squares out in four rows of four, alternating the colourways, in a pleasing pattern. Join them together in rows of four, stitching 12mm (½in) in from the edge. Press the seams open. Pin the rows together, carefully aligning the seams. Sew together, leaving an identical seam allowance.

3 When the whole square has been completed, press the seams open. As backing, cut a piece of coordinating fabric to the same size as the seat top. Then, with right sides together, pin the cover to the backing fabric.

4 Cut the 2.5cm (1in) wide length of ribbon in two and fold each piece in half. With the fold outermost, sandwich the ribbons between the layers, and pin in place 2.5cm (1in) in from either edge of one side.

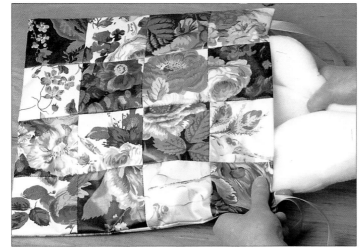

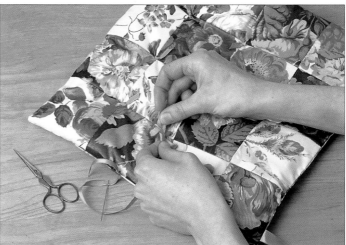

5 Sew around three sides of the square and turn through. Cut three layers of wadding (batting) the same size as the seat cover and tack (baste) together. Place inside the cover and slip stitch the fourth side closed.

6 Thread a large-eyed needle with the thin ribbon and push through the seat cover, close to the corner of one square. Bring up to the right side, on the other side of the intersection, and tie the ends in a tight reef knot. Clip back to 2cm (¾in) and repeat across the whole seat cover.

Heart Cushion (Pillow)

This romantic lacy cushion (pillow) would be equally suitable as a present for a bride, or as a valentine gift. The design of interlocked hearts is machine-quilted on to raw silk, and emphasized with the addition of tiny seed-pearl beads. The edge is finished with a ruffle of antique lace. It could be made as a precious keepsake, using remnants of fabric and trimmings left from a wedding dress, and used as a ring cushion (pillow).

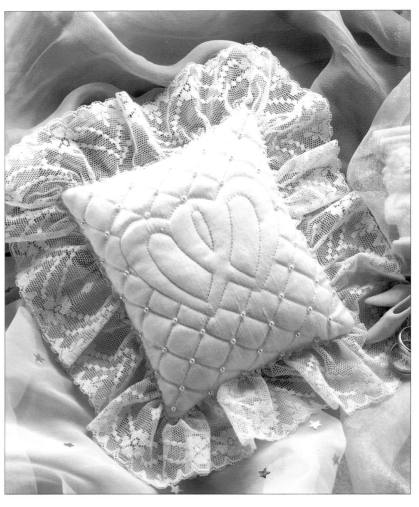

MATERIALS
Tracing paper; pencil; thin cardboard; ruler
15 x 35cm (6 x 14in) piece of cream silk
Dressmaker's fading pen; dressmaker's pins
18 x 20cm (7 x 8in) piece of polyester
  wadding (batting); 18 x 20cm (7 x 8in)
  piece of white cotton fabric
Sewing machine; matching sewing thread
122cm (48in) length of 5cm (2in) lace
Polyester toy stuffing; tiny seed-pearl beads

1 Trace the heart motif on to thin cardboard and cut out. From the silk fabric cut a 15 x 18cm (6 x 7in) rectangle. Using a dressmaker's fading pen, rule two diagonal lines to mark the centre. Place the template in the middle of the cross and draw round it, then draw a 15mm (⅝ in) grid across the rest of the fabric.

2 Tack (baste) the cushion (pillow) top to the wadding and back with cotton fabric to prevent it snagging in the machine. Thread the machine with matching thread and stitch over the grid and heart outline. (The fading pen lines will disappear in a few hours.) Trim back the excess wadding (batting) and square off the edges.

3 Cut a second piece of silk to the same size, pin to the right side of the quilted piece and stitch together, leaving a space. Clip the corners, turn through, and fill with stuffing. Slip stitch the space closed.

4 Join the ends of the lace and run a line of gathering stitches along the straight edge. Pin to the corners of the cushion (pillow), even out the gathers and over-stitch. Sew seed pearls where quilting lines cross.

Hexagonal Pincushion

The all-over mosaic effect of hexagonal patches is surprisingly easy to achieve, as the shapes do not have any sharp angles to be joined. Six-sided shapes are usually worked over a paper backing, rather than being sewn together with straight stitch, and this way of assembling must be used when working on a small scale. The miniature patchwork technique could be extended to make a tiny quilt for a doll's house.

MATERIALS
Isometric graph paper
Ruler; pen; thin cardboard
Scraps of cotton fabric; cotton sewing thread
Small quantity of polyester wadding (batting)
Embroidery scissors: rocaille beads

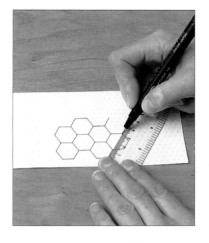

1 Following the triangular grid printed on the isometric graph paper, use a pen and ruler to mark out fourteen hexagons with 10mm (⅜in) sides. Cut out accurately. These are the backing papers.

2 Draw a hexagon on thin cardboard to use as a template for cutting the fabric: it should measure approximately 6mm (¼in) greater all round than the backing paper. Use the template as a guide to cut out the patches. Tack each patch centrally on to a backing paper, then fold over and tack down the seam allowance, making sure that the corners are tidy.

3 Sew the patches together by overstitching the outside edges, picking up just two threads of fabric on each side with each stitch and holding them with right sides facing. Join into two rosettes of seven hexagons each.

4 Press lightly and remove the backing papers. With wrong sides facing, overstitch rosettes together, leaving a small space at one side. Stuff the pincushion with polyester wadding (batting), using the point of a pair of scissors to ease the fibre carefully right into the corners. Oversew the space and then sew rocaille beads around the outside edge to make a decorative border.

Appliqué

Appliqué is the simple process of stitching one fabric onto another. The application of fabrics, however, takes many forms. It can be purely functional or more highly decorative, and ranges from patching a worn knee on a garment to combining specially chosen materials to produce attractive, soft furnishings for the home. The end results can be simply stunning!

Star-Fruit Panel

The exotic shapes and hues of tropical star fruit and passion fruit are the source of this lively design, which uses the innovative technique of reverse appliqué. Several pieces of bright felt are stitched together and then cut back, one at a time, to reveal the underlying layers. Extra colour and detail are added with machine and hand stitching, using toning embroidery threads. The textured stitches give a sculptured feel to the finished piece, could be framed or made into a cushion (pillow).

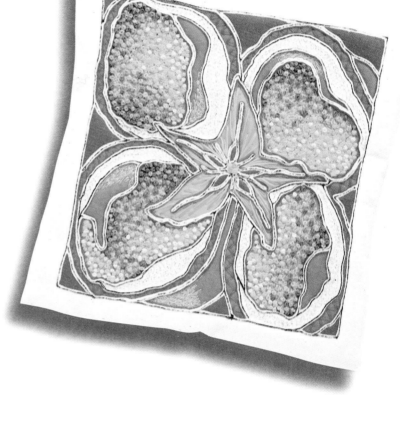

MATERIALS

Transfer pencil, or dressmaker's chalk or carbon; pins
Tracing paper
35cm (14in) square of white felt; dressmaker's pins
30cm (12in) squares of purple, yellow, green, pink felt
Cotton sewing thread
Sewing machine; pointed sharp embroidery scissors
Machine embroidery thread in a selection of toning
  colours and black
Perlé embroidery thread in white, yellow, green and pink

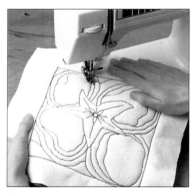

1 Enlarge and trace the design from the template and transfer it on to the centre of the white felt square. Pin, then tack all the felt together, with white on top, then purple, pink, green and yellow. Thread the sewing machine with black thread and sew over the outline in straight stitch. Finish off all the ends securely.

2 Cut into the layers of felt, referring to the main picture as a guide. Keep as close to the black stitched line as possible without cutting into it, and leave an equal amount of white felt along either side of the line.

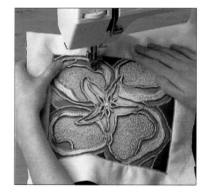

3 Once all the layers have been cut, extra stitched detail can be worked into the design. Set the sewing machine to the widest zigzag, lower the feed dog, and work random stitches in toning threads over the coloured areas of the panel. This will enhance the effect of the varying layers and heights of the felt.

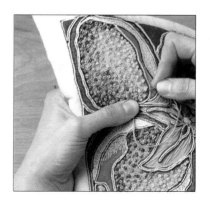

4 Work the fine detail by hand in perlé thread. Use two shades of each colour to give the appearance of real depth. Work the insides of the passion fruit with French knots and fill in the star fruit with radiating straight stitches.

Cornucopia

The cornucopia is an ancient symbol representing "abundance in everything desired". This felt picture is a reinterpretation of a design from an appliquéd bridal quilt, which was made in the American seaport of Baltimore in the mid-nineteenth century. The bedcovers made there are instantly recognizable by their lavish use of colour and intricate patterns: the women who made them always had access to the latest fabrics and designs from the traders and importers of the town. This modern version uses iron-on bonding and felt, and is quick and easy to make.

MATERIALS
Tracing paper
Fine felt-tip pen; pencil
Paper-backed fusible bonding
Small pieces of felt in yellow, orange, red, light green, dark green, light blue, dark blue and lilac
Pointed embroidery scissors
35 x 41cm (14 x 16in) piece of white felt

1 Copy the design outline from the template, and enlarge as required, bearing in mind that the finished design will be reversed. Referring to the main photograph, work out which shapes are cut from each colour of felt. Trace all the elements for each colour on to a separate piece of fusible bonding, drawing on to the paper-covered side.

3 Peel off the backing paper from the iron-on fusible bonding. Following the manufacturer's instructions, begin to iron the shapes on to the backing felt, starting with the the cornucopia. Use the wrong side of the traced main template outline as a guide. Build up the bottom layers first, then the stalks, stems and leaves.

2 Place the relevant tracings on the coloured felts, paper side up. Cover with a damp cloth and press on. Cut out all the shapes.

4 Iron on the apple, pear and the main flowers, then add the buds, strawberries, grapes and coloured dots.

Goose Shopping Bag

A remnant of hard-wearing checked furnishing fabric is used to make this shopping bag, which is decorated with an endearing goose, complete with its own egg. The goose's body is cut from unbleached plain calico or cotton fabric and the wing feather patterns are indicated using lines of running stitch. A scrap of bright orange chintz is used for the feet and beak. The broad handles of the bag are comfortable to hold when it is laden with shopping. The finished bag measures 50 x 38cm (20 x 15in).

MATERIALS
25 x 30cm (10 x 12in) piece of unbleached plain calico or cotton fabric
50 x 75cm (20 x 30in) piece of checked furnishing fabric, plus 50 x 25cm (20 x 10in) for the handles
Tracing paper
Soft pencil or water-soluble pen
Stranded embroidery thread in dark brown and tan
Scrap of bright orange chintz
Matching cotton sewing thread
Small piece of multicoloured check fabric for the egg
Sewing machine; pins

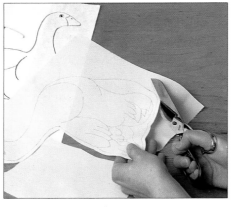

1 Enlarge the template as necessary. Place the calico over the outline and trace the main body on to the fabric with a soft pencil or water-soluble pen. This is the wrong side of the work. Carefully leaving a 6mm (¼in) allowance around the edge, then cut out the goose.

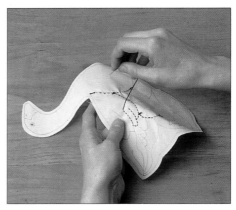

2 Using three strands of the dark brown embroidery thread, work over the wing and feather outlines with lines of small neat running stitches. Mark the pupil of the eye with satin stitch and a circle of running stitch. Start and finish all the threads on the upper side of the fabric.

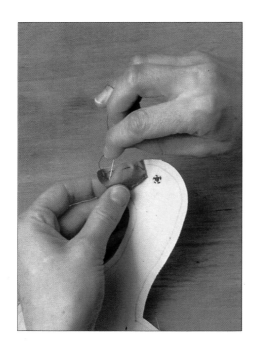

3 Turn the goose over so that it is facing to the left. Cut the beak from orange chintz, allowing an extra 6mm (¼in) seam allowance. Turn under the two inside edges and stitch in place on to the head. Clip the curves around the seam allowance and tack (baste) under.

4 Cut out the feet, allowing an extra 6mm (¼in); tack (baste) this under and press. Tack (baste) the left foot in place under the body, then pin the goose on to the front right side of the main bag fabric. Sew the goose down with tan running stitch.

5 Pin on the second foot and sew down with running stitch. Cut an egg shape from multicoloured checked fabric, tack (baste) the edges under and sew in place in the bottom right-hand corner.

6 Cut two strips 12.5 x 51cm (5 x 20in) each to form the handles. Stitch each along the long edge, then turn through and press.

Fold the bag fabric in half, with the appliqué on the inside, then sew along the side and bottom edges. Turn right side out, and fold under 2.5cm (1in) all around the top edge. Press, then turn under another 2.5cm (1in) and sew down with two lines of straight stitch. Neaten the ends of the handles and sew firmly in place.

Mosaic Cushion (Pillow)

1 Cut out random geometric shapes from the fabric scraps, selecting the most interesting patterned areas. These should be a mixture of triangles and four- or five-sided shapes. Turn under 6mm (¼in) along each straight side, folding the surplus fabric at the points back on itself. Tack down, then press each shape.

2 Fold the background fabric in half. Place appliqué pieces on one side. Leave a clear 2.5cm (1in) border around the edge and position the shapes so that they fit together in a pleasing pattern. Take some time to move the pieces around to find the best arrangement. Pin in place.

Appliqué shapes with sharp angles or pointed corners are not always straightforward to stitch, so this cushion (pillow) cover is a good way to practise them. Collect together assorted scraps of blue-and-white printed fabric and sew them on to a dark background for a mosaic effect that resembles fragments of china.

3 Stitch the shapes to the background fabric with white sewing thread using small tidy overstitches. Be sure that any surplus fabric has been tucked under at the corners. Fold the fabric in half with right sides together, then sew around two sides, leaving a 12mm (½in) seam allowance. Insert the cushion (pillow) pad, then slip stitch the third side closed with matching thread.

MATERIALS

Scraps of blue-and-white printed fabric
Cotton tacking (basting) thread
33 x 63cm (13 x 25in) piece of plain chintz fabric
  for the background
Dressmaker's pins' white cotton sewing thread
30cm (12in) cushion (pillow) pad
Matching cotton sewing thread

Shoe Bag

A
ll kinds of textiles can be combined to produce interesting appliqué effects. For this project, an ordinary striped linen tea (dish) towel is transformed into a practical shoe bag by the simple process of sewing on bands of ribbon. A wide range of printed ribbons is now available – the ones chosen for this project all have a nautical theme, which is re-emphasized by the brass eyelets and the thick white cotton drawstring.

MATERIALS
Striped linen tea (dish) towel
90cm (36in) lengths of patterned ribbon
Sewing machine; matching cotton sewing thread
10 x 90cm (4 x 36in) piece of lightweight iron-on
  interfacing
Dressmaker's pins
Waterproof lining (optional); brass eyelets
90cm (36in) length of white cord or extra ribbon

1 Using the stripes as a guide, sew the ribbon on to the tea (dish) towel with a wide zigzag. Start each line of stitching from the same end so that the ribbon does not pucker.

2 On the wrong side, iron the interfacing along one long edge to provide support for the eyelets. Fold the tea towel in half with the appliqué on the inside. Pin and stitch the side and bottom edges together. Fold under 5cm (2in) around the top edge and press. A waterproof lining could be added at this stage to make the bag into a soap bag.

3 Following the manufacturer's instructions, hammer in the eyelets at evenly spaced intervals around the top edge of the bag.
Thread the cord or ribbon through the eyelets and tie the two ends together.

Oven Glove (Mitt)

A confident handling of unrestrained colour along with the graphic strength of the egg cup motif, makes this essentially practical oven glove (mitt) a decorative kitchen accessory. A pattern of moons and stars makes a pleasing constrast on the other side of the glove (mitt). The main shape is cut from cotton gingham and quilted by hand, then contrasting perlé embroidery threads are used to emphasize the appliqué design.

MATERIALS

Tracing paper; pencil
30 x 41cm (12 x 16in) piece of heat-resistant
  wadding (batting)
30 x 70cm (12 x 28in) piece of gingham
Water-soluble fabric pen or dressmaker's chalk or
  carbon; ruler
Perlé embroidery thread in a selection of colours
Scraps of fabric for the appliqué
Fabric adhesive; matching cotton sewing thread
Contrasting fabric for cuff; ribbon for the loop

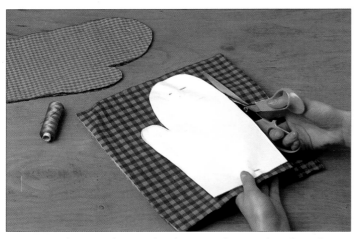

1 Trace the template and enlarge to fit your hand easily. Sandwich the wadding (batting) between two pieces of checked fabric, pin the pattern in place and cut out two hand shapes. Tack (baste) the layers together.

2 Using a water-soluble fabric pen or with dressmaker's chalk or carbon, rule diagonal lines across each half of the glove (mitt) to make even squares. Sew over this grid with a contrasting embroidery thread.

3 Cut out the appliqué pieces from scraps of fabric and, using fabric adhesive, fix them in place. Use the template as a guide for cutting the egg cup and spoon shapes for the back of the glove (mitt), and make a more random pattern on the palm side.

4 Take the fabric shapes and, with brightly coloured perlé embroidery thread, sew the pieces, using decorative stitches.

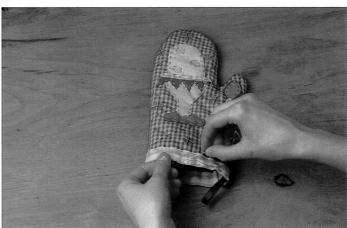

5 With right sides facing, sew the two pieces together, leaving a seam allowance of 12mm (½in). Clip the curves and turn through.

6 Cut a 7.5 x 25cm (3 x 10in) strip of contrasting fabric to trim the cuff. Fold in half lengthways and press. Turn under the raw edges, to the centre, and press. Place the fabric around the open edge of the glove and stitch in place. Sew a loop of ribbon to the inside of the glove (mitt) for hanging.

Apron

This bright and cheerful cotton drill apron is bound to enliven the most mundane household task, from tending to the dishes or polishing the car to washing and dusting. Iron-on fusible bonding is used to attach the main motifs, but the smaller shapes are fixed in place with time-saving fabric adhesive. The neck loop and ties are made from one continuous length of tape, which means that it will always adjust to fit the individual wearer.

MATERIALS
75 x 100cm (30 x 40in) piece of fabric for the apron
Dressmaker's pins
Sewing machine; matching machine sewing thread
12.5 x 115cm (5 x 45in) piece of fabric for the tie
Tracing paper; pencil; iron-on fusible bonding
Perlé embroidery thread in a selection of colours
Scraps of fabric for the appliqué shapes
51cm (20in) square of fabric for the pocket
Fabric adhesive
Safety pin
Bias binding; rick-rack braid (trim)

1 Make the apron shape by cutting away two curved shapes from the top of the main fabric, leaving a 25cm (8in) straight edge in the centre. Stitch a double hem along each of the four straight sides. Fold under a seam allowance of 6mm (¼in) along the two curved edges and press down. Turn under again, then pin and stitch down 2cm (¾in) from the edge, to form a channel for the tie.

2 Cut two strips of fabric, each 6.5 x 115cm (2½ x 45in), and join to make the tie. Fold in half along the length, with wrong sides together, and press. Unfold the fabric, fold the edges lengthways into the centre and press. Fold back together along the original crease, press and pin in place, turning in the two ends. Machine stitch along both sides of the tie to secure.

3 Enlarge the template and trace the large cactus shapes on to the paper side of the fusible bonding. Iron on to the chosen fabric and cut out. Using the main picture as a guide, cut circles and stars from contrasting scraps of cotton fabric. Glue in place with fabric adhesive.

4 Cut two pieces of fabric for the pocket, each measuring approximately 28 x 35 x 48cm (11 x 14 x 19in). Sew together with right sides facing, leaving a small space at one side. Clip the corners and turn through. Stitch the space together with slip stitch and press down.

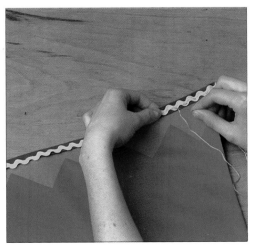

5 Cut a length of coloured fabric with a wide zigzag edge and attach it to the top of the apron pocket with fabric adhesive. Stitch a piece of coloured bias binding along the same edge. Finish off with a length of ric-rac braid (trim), sewn down with running stitch.

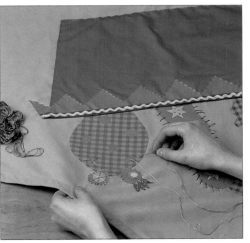

6 Hand stitch the pocket to the apron with contrasting embroidery thread. Peel the backing from the cactus shapes and, with a damp cloth, iron into place. The spikes are sewn on with green thread using random straight stitches. Attach a safety pin to the tie and thread through the channels, leaving a loop

75

Nightdress Case

Padded appliqué has a luxurious appearance, especially when worked with lavish satins and taffetas. Printed or patterned motifs are stitched on to a backing fabric, then stuffed with wadding (batting), to give extra depth to the finished piece. This glamorous nightdress case is lined with iron-on quilting, which is quick and convenient to use, and trimmed with silkcord and tassels.

MATERIALS

38 x 83cm (15 x 33in) piece of iron-on quilting
41 x 140cm (16 x 55in) piece of taffeta
Remnant of printed fabric with cherub pattern
Dressmaker's pins
Matching cotton sewing thread; sewing machine
Small piece of polyester wadding (batting)
140cm (55in) length of heavy cord; 2 tassels

1 Using a damp cloth, press the quilting to the taffeta, 41cm (16in) from one short end, with 12mm (½in) at each side. The larger flap of taffeta will later be folded over to form the back of the bag's decorated front flap.

2 Cut out two cherub motifs from the printed fabric.

3 Position the cherubs on the right side of the cover flap and sew in place with satin stitch, in thread to match the main fabric.

4 Turn over, and carefully cut a slit through both the quilting and taffeta, along the length of each motif. Use the point of a pair of scissors to push small amounts of wadding (batting) into the shape, being careful not to overstuff. Sew up the slit, and fold the loose end of taffeta back to cover the quilting. Pin the two sides together, then sew with satin stitch to make a flap.

5 Fold the spare taffeta at the other end back over the quilting, then fold the lower part in half to form the main bag. Pin the sides together, then sew with satin stitch. Trim the raw edges and hand stitch the cord around the sides and flap. Finish off the bottom corners by sewing on the tassels.

Notice (Bulletin) Board

New textile processes are always being developed and can be incorporated with traditional ways of working to produce dramatic effects. This *trompe-l'oeil* notice (bulletin) board is decorated with a collage of brightly coloured postcards and uses an inventive technique to transfer the images on to cloth. The transfer solution is available from most craft shops.

MATERIALS

Image-transfer solution
6 colour photocopies of postcards or photo
White cotton fabric; Cork board plus green
*   felt or baize to cover*
Iron-on fusible bonding
Sewing machine; machine embroidery
*   thread in gold; embroidery hoop*
Drawing pins; thumb tacks

1 Following the instructions, transfer the photocopied images on to the white fabric. Most processes suggest that the image dries for 24 hours and is then fixed with a hot iron.

2 Cut the green felt or baize to fit the board, allowing 5cm (2in) extra around each edge. Trim the surplus fabric from around the transferred images.

3 Cut a piece of iron-on fusible bonding the same size as each of the postcard images. Iron the adhesive side on to the reverse of each image, then peel off the backing paper. Arrange the postcards and iron on to the felt, using a piece of cloth to protect the images.

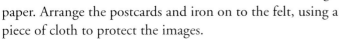

4 Put the felt in an embroidery hoop and machine stitch lines of straight or satin stitch in gold around each image. Fix the felt to the board using tacks, at the back. Fasten lengths of ribbon across the board to form a lattice, securing the intersections with drawing pins.

Tartan (Plaid) Throw

The informality of floral chintz and the geometric patterns of tartan fabrics work well together, and the combination has a traditional country-house feel to it. This versatile throw is made from a length of woven furnishing-weight tartan (plaid) with a lavish swag of flowers and leaves appliquéd across one corner, and a smaller arrangement at the opposite end. The flowered fabric came from an upholsterer's old sample book – a good source of different patterns and colourways.

MATERIALS
Remnants of floral chintz fabric
90cm (36in) iron-on fusible bonding
137 x 152cm (54 x 60in) piece of woven tartan (plaid) furnishing fabric
Dressmaker's pins
Sewing machine
Various matching machine sewing threads
Decorative furnishing braid (optional)

1 Sort through the remnants of the chintz fabric and select the most eye-catching leaves and flowers. Cut a rough shape from fusible bonding for each and iron on to the back of the fabric. Cut out, leaving a narrow margin around the edge.

2 Peel off the backing paper. Lay the flowers out on the tartan fabric, taking some time to arrange them into a pleasing pattern. Overlap some of the individual shapes and use separate leaves to fill in any spaces.

3 Once a final arrangement has been decided, iron the shapes down, being careful not to move them out of place. It may help to pin the flowers down before pressing them.

4 Thread the sewing machine with green thread and set to a wide close satin stitch. Sew around all the raw leaf edges, varying the shades of the thread to match the different fabrics. Use pinks and reds to edge the flowers.

5 When the appliqué is complete, trim the tartan (plaid) fabric so that the edges are square and fray along each side to form a narrow fringe. Some fabrics may not unravel easily, in which case a decorative furnishing braid could be used to trim the throw.

Bolster Pillow

Appliqué can be used to subtle effect by combining fabrics in a similar colour range, but with contrasting textures. The bolster cover is constructed from reverse appliqué, in which two pieces of fabric are stitched together and parts of the upper layer cut away to reveal the cloth below. The pillow would fit into any interior design scheme and look at home in an understated modern environment, or piled on a sofa amidst brocade and velvet cushions.

MATERIALS
65 x 90cm (26 x 36in) white cotton fabric
51 x 65cm (20 x 26in) cream cotton fabric
Dressmaker's pins; cotton tacking (basting) thread
Dressmaker's chalk or carbon
Thin cardboard; pencil
White cotton sewing thread; sewing machine
45cm (18in) bolster pad
90cm (36in) length of ribbon

1 Cut a 51 x 65cm (20 x 26in) piece of white fabric and place over the cream fabric, aligning the weave. Pin together, then tack (baste) a grid of 9cm (3½in) squares across the surface. Enlarge and transfer the template design on to thin cardboard and cut out. Draw the triangular pattern on to the fabric, reversing the template either side of the tacked line.

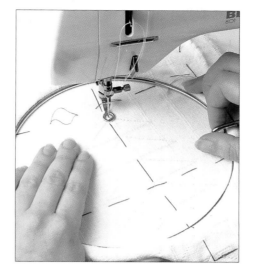

2 With white cotton sewing thread, machine straight stitch over the chalk marks to outline the triangles.

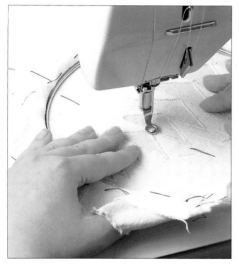

3 Carefully cut away the top layer of fabric within the stitching. Set the machine to zigzag and work satin stitch over the straight stitch to cover the raw edges. Repeat until the entire cloth has been appliquéd.

4 Cut the rest of the white fabric in two long strips, and mark a zigzag border, 10cm (4in) deep, along one long edge of each. Sew with straight stitch and cut out close to the stitching. Work satin stitch over the raw edges.

5 Sew one frilled piece to each end of the main piece and fold in half lengthways, with right sides together. Join along the side seam, leaving a seam allowance of 2cm (¾in). Press the seams open and turn right side out.

6 Insert the pad into the pillow cover and keep in place by tying each end of the case with a length of ribbon, like a Christmas cracker.

Knitting

Hand knitting is a skill that can be enjoyed at many levels and most people remember with great affection making their first multicoloured scarf. The projects in this section range from simple cushions, hats and baby booties to more demanding, beautiful designs in a range of exciting styles.

Cable Cushion (Pillow)

The hand-knitted jerseys (sweaters) worn by fishing communities evolved a distinctive functional style over many years. They were made from heavy-duty wool, still impregnated with lanolin, to keep them waterproof and to stand up to hard wear. This attractive cushion (pillow) combines the newest indigo-dyed cotton yarns with long-established patterns; the moss stitch and cable pattern are reminiscent of Guernsey jumpers (sweaters) from the Channel Islands. The natural blue indigo dye is also used for denim; so, like jeans, this cushion (pillow) will fade with wear and use. The finished cushion (pillow) measures 30cm (12in) square.

(NOTE: Cotton yarn has very little "give". To ensure an even tension (gauge), knit as far towards the tips of the needles as you can.)

MATERIALS

100g (4oz) indigo cotton yarn in double knitting weight
Pair of 4.00mm knitting needles
Cable needle
33cm (13in) square of dark blue needlecord (pinwale corduroy)
33cm (13in) square of blue brushed cotton fabric
Matching cotton sewing thread
30cm (12in) square cushion (pillow) pad
Cardboard

1 The twisted cable pattern is worked by slipping three stitches on to a cable needle and holding it at the front of the work while knitting the next three stitches from the left-hand needle. The three stitches on the cable needle are then knitted. This is abbreviated as (C6f) for "cable six forward".

2 TO MAKE UP With right sides facing, sew the needlecord and brushed cotton fabric squares together around three sides, leaving a seam allowance of 12mm (½in). Press the seams and turn right side out. Slip stitch the knitted panel on to the cotton lining, using the indigo yarn.

3 Insert the cushion (pillow) pad and slip stitch the fourth side closed.

4 Make each looped tassel by winding a length of yarn round a 7.5cm (3in) wide piece of cardboard about 20 times. Slip off and sew the loop on to the corner as shown, binding the tassel head close to the stitching.

INSTRUCTIONS

Cast on 60 sts.
Row 1 K1, P1 to end.
Row 2 P1, K1 to end.
Row 3 as row 1;
Row 4 as row 2.
Row 5 K1, P1, K1, P1, P7, C6f, P7, (K1, P1) 6 times, P7, C6f, P7, K1,(P1, K1, P1
Row 6 P1, K1 P1, K1, K7, P6, K7 (P1, K1) 6 times, K7, P6, K7, P1, K1, P1, K1.
Row 7 K1, P1, K1, P1, P7, K6, P7,

(K1, P1) 6 times, P7, K6, P7, K1, P1, K1, P1.
Row 8 P1, K1, P1, K1, P5, K2, P6, K2, P5 (K1, P1) 6 times, P5, K2, P6, K2, P5, P1, K1, P1, K1.
Row 9 K1, P1, K1, P1, K5, P2, K6, P2, K5, (K1, P1) 6 times, K5, P2, K6, P2, K5, K1, P1, K1, P1.
Row 10 P1, K1, P1, K1, P5, K2, P6, K2, P5 (P1, K1) 6 times, P5, K2, P6, K2, P5, P1, K1, P1, K1.
Repeat rows 5-10 twelve times. Repeat rows 1-4 (80 rows). Cast off.

Basket Edging

Knitted lace is hard wearing, adaptable and can be worked in a variety of sizes and textures. The basket edging shown here is made on a large scale using unbleached craft cotton, but could easily be made on very fine needles with perlé crochet cotton or 2-ply Shetland wool to make a collar or cuff trimming for a garment. This traditional pattern is known as "ten stitch", as it is worked on a foundation of ten stitches.

MATERIALS
Cotton yarn in double knitting weight
Pair of 3.50mm knitting needles
Basket
Tapestry needle

1 The open lacy effect of the basket edging is created by repeating a simple stitch pattern: wind the yarn forward once around the needle to make an extra stitch, then knit the next two stitches together. This is abbreviated in the instructions as (yrn, K2 tog).

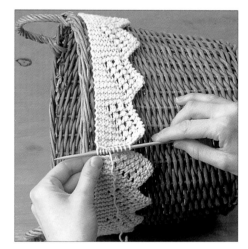

2 Cast off when the lace is long enough to fit around the basket, ending on row 14 so that the zigzag edge is complete. Join the two edges together neatly and fit the edging around the rim of the basket.

INSTRUCTIONS
Cast on 10 st. Rows 1-14 form the pattern.

Row 1 sl 1, K3 (yrn, K2 tog) twice, yrn, K2.

Row 2 and every even-numbered row, K to end.

Row 3 sl 1, K4 (yrn, K2 tog) twice, yrn, K2.

Row 5 sl 1, K5 (yrn, K2 tog) twice, yrn, K2.

Row 7 sl 1, K6 (yrn, K2 tog) twice, yrn, K2.

Row 9 sl 1, K7 (yrn, K2 tog) twice, yrn, K2.

Row 11 sl 1, K8 (yrn, K2 tog) twice, yrn, K2.

Row 13 sl 1, K to end.

Row 14 cast off 6 sts, K to end (10 sts).

3 Sew in place using a tapestry needle. Pass the needle right through the basket from one side to the other, using small tidy stitches and being careful not to pull the thread too tightly.

Shetland Lace Scarf

Shetland lies between Scotland and Scandinavia, and consists of some 100 islands, set at the crossroads of the North Sea and the North Atlantic. The hardy strain of Shetland sheep has long been bred on the islands, and for over 500 years their fleece has been spun and made into garments. The multicoloured Fair Isle pullovers are famous, but the finest of the single- and two-ply yarns are knitted into lace shawls and scarves. This pattern is inspired by the crashing waves of the seas that surround the islands. The finished scarf measures 90 x 25cm (36 x10in).

MATERIALS
2-ply Shetland wool:
  25g (1oz) in white
  15g (½ oz) each in blue, pink and lilac
Pair of 3.00mm knitting needles
Tapestry needle

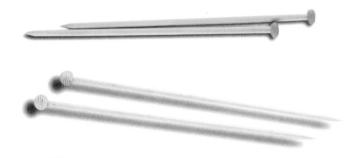

TENSION (GAUGE)

Using 3.00mm needles, 10 pattern rows measure 2.5cm (1in).
Cast on 75 st in white.
Row 1 K2, K2 tog (K3, yfwd, K1, yfwd, K3, K3 tog) to last 11 sts, K3, yfwd, K1, yfwd, K3, K2 tog, K2.
Row 2 K to end.
These two rows form the pattern: repeat five times more and then continue the pattern using the following colour sequence, breaking off the yarn at the end of each stripe.
*
**
2 rows blue
2 rows lilac
2 rows pink
2 rows white
2 rows pink
2 rows lilac
2 rows blue
**
8 rows white
Repeat from ** to ** once
8 rows white
Repeat from ** to ** to complete coloured wave
*
24 rows white
2 rows blue
24 rows white
Repeat coloured wave from * to * once
24 rows white
2 rows blue
24 rows white
Repeat coloured wave from * to * once
12 rows white to finish.

1 It is important not to work too tightly when knitting the three stitches together, so that the right-hand needle can pass easily through all the loops.

2 Cast off loosely and darn in all the loose ends.

3 Pin out both ends of the scarf so that the edges form peaks, then press lightly with a damp cloth. Allow to dry away from direct heat and sunlight.

Baby Wrap

This innovative baby wrap is warm and comfortable for winter outings. It is worked in double knitting yarn and lined with soft cotton. The pattern of geometric bands and child-like figures is knitted from an easy-to-follow chart. The front and back are made separately, then joined together, leaving the convenient zip (zipper) opening along the lower edge. The finished garment measures 51cm (20in) from collar to hem and 28cm (11in) across the chest.

MATERIALS
50g (2oz) double knitting yarn each in lilac, beige,
  purple, turquoise and dark green
Pair each of 3.25mm and 4.50mm knitting needles
3.25mm circular needle
Stitch holder
2 buttons
2 x 41cm (16in) zips (zippers)
60cm (24in) square of fabric for the lining
Matching cotton sewing thread

BACK
Using 4.50mm needles, cast on 68 sts in lilac.
Row 1 K to end
Row 2 P to end.
Row 3 inc 1, K to end, inc 1.
Work the pattern from the chart, increasing 1 st at each end of the 5th, 7th and 9th rows (76 sts). Carry the contrast yarn across the back of the knitting.
Row 54 dec 1 st at each end of this and following 4th rows until 60 sts remain. Work 12 rows from pattern.
Row 94 K to end of row and inc 20 sts.
Row 95 P to end of row and inc 20 sts. Continue to follow the chart, knitting on these 100 sts for the 17 remaining rows of the pattern. Knit 5 rows lilac. Cast off.

FRONT
Work as for the back until row 105, then decrease for the left shoulder and neck shaping, using the chart as a guide.
Row 106 K45, then put centre 10 sts on to st holder. Dec 1 at neck edge, K to end. Working on these 44 sts –
Row 107 dec 1 at end of row (neck edge).
Row 108 work row without decreasing.
Row 109 dec 1 st at end of row (neck edge).
Row 110 dec 1 st at beg of row.
Rows 111 – 115 work remainder of pattern, and knit 5 rows lilac.
Cast off. Reverse instructions for right shoulder and neck opening.

TO MAKE UP

Sew in the ends and press lightly. Set marks in contrasting yarn 27 sts from the cuff edge on the left-hand side of the front and back, at the centre front and back at the cast-on edge and 5 rows up from the cast-on edge back and front.

2 SEAMS With right sides together, sew along the shoulder seams to the neck edge on the right-hand side and to the marker on the left-hand side.

1 CUFFS Pick up 40 sts on size 3.25mm needles and work 8 rows K1, P1 rib. Cast off rib-wise.

3 NECK Pick up stitches round the neck with the circular needle, starting at the left-hand top: 4 sts along rib; 8 sts along neck edge; 10 sts from holder; 8 sts along neck edge; 20 sts along back neck; 4 sts along rib. Rib these sts for 4 rows and cast off. Sew buttons on to the shoulder fastening.

4 TO SEW IN THE ZIPS Pin the zip (zippers) in the opening at the bottom, then stitch in place to the markers on the lower edge of the front and back.

5 TO LINE Cut two shapes from the lining fabric 4cm (1½in) larger than the finished knitted wrap. Join at the shoulder, under the arm and along the side seams. With wrong sides together, sew the lining to the inside of the wrap at the cuffs, neck edges and along each open side.

TO FINISH THE NECK OPENING

Back Pick up 13 sts along from the marker to the neck edge. Rib 3 rows and cast off.

FRONT

Pick up 13 sts from the marker to the neck edge.
Rows 1 and 2 work in K1, P1 rib.
Row 3 K1, cast off 1, rib 4, cast off 1, rib 4.
Row 4 rib 4, cast on 1, rib 4, cast on 1, K1.
Cast off.

Baby Mittens and Baby Shoes

Knitted bootees or shoes are a popular present for a new baby, and a first pair is often kept as a souvenir. These brightly striped T-bar shoes will fit from newborn up to four months old and are worked in a practical, washable cotton yarn. The matching mittens are made in a basic design with minimal shaping and would be suitable for a baby of up to nine months.

BABY MITTENS MATERIALS
Small quantity of double knitting yarn in pink,
  orange and yellow
Pair each of 3.00mm and 3.50mm knitting needles
Tapestry needle

1 TO MAKE THE CORDS Cut six 45cm (18in) strands of yarn, two each in pink, orange and yellow. Knot together at one end, leaving 2.5cm (1in) of yarn to form a tassel. Secure the knot with a weight, or pin to a fixed object, then plait (braid) to the end. Make a knot 2.5cm (1in) from the end of the finished plait (braid). Brush and trim the tassels.

TENSION (GAUGE)
Using 3.50mm needles, 21 sts and 30 rows measure 10cm (4in) – st st.
Begin at the cuff. Using 3.00mm needles and pink yarn, cast on 34 sts.
Row 1 K2, P2 to end.
Row 2 P2, K2 to end.
Repeat 1st and 2nd rows 8 times more. Change to orange and yellow yarn and 3.50mm needles. Work in the stripe pattern throughout (2 rows orange, 2 rows yellow).
Eyelet row (K2, yfwd, K2 tog) to end.
Starting with a P row, work 19 rows st st.
Dec Row K1 (K2 tog tbl, K12, K2 tog) twice, K1.
Next row P to end.
Dec row K1 (K2 tog tbl, K10, K2 tog) twice, K1.
(30 sts) Cast off.

2 TO MAKE UP With wrong sides together, slip stitch the top seam using the end of the yellow yarn.

3 Turn right side out and stitch along the side seam.

4 Use pink yarn to join cuff. Thread cords through the eyelets.

Row 5 K1, inc 1, K13, inc 1, K1, inc 1, K13, inc 1, K1.
Row 7 K1, inc 1, K15, inc 1, K1, inc 1, K15, inc 1, K1.
Row 9 K1, inc 1, K17, inc 1, K1, inc 1, K17, inc 1, K1.
Row 11 K1, inc 1, K19, inc 1, K1, inc 1, K19, inc 1, K1.
Row 12 K to end.

Change to orange and yellow yarn and work the upper part of the shoe in the stripe pattern throughout (2 rows orange, 2 rows yellow).

Row 13 K17, sl 1, K1, psso, K11, K2 tog, K17.
Row 14 and every even-numbered row, P to end.
Row 15 K17, sl 1, K1, psso, K9, K2 tog, K17.
Row 17 K17, sl 1, K1, psso, K7, K2 tog, K17.
Row 19 K17, sl 1, K1, psso, K5, K2 tog, K17.
Row 20 P to end.
Row 21 K9.

Cast off 9, K5 (including st on needle after casting off) cast off 9, K9. Beginning with a P row, work 4 rows st st on these 9 sts. Cast off.

BABY SHOES MATERIALS
Oddments of double knitting yarn in pink, orange and yellow
Pair of 3.00mm knitting needles
2 matching buttons or beads; tapestry needle

TENSION (GAUGE)
Using 3.00mm needles, 21sts and 30 rows measures 10cm (4in) – (st st).
Begin with the sole. Using pink, cast on 25 sts.
Row 1 K1, inc 1, K9, inc 1, K1, inc 1, K9, inc 1, K1.
Row 2 and every even-numbered row, P to end.
Row 3 K1, inc 1, K11, inc 1, K1, inc 1, K11, inc 1, K1.

TO MAKE THE ANKLE STRAP
Return to the remaining 9 sts, cast on 12 sts (on to the same needle as 9 sts). P across these sts, then P across the group of 9 sts (21 sts).
Work 4 rows st st. Cast off.

TO MAKE THE T-BAR
Return to the centre 5 sts. Beginning with a P row, work 15 rows st st. Cast off.

SECOND SHOE
Make as for the first shoe, reversing the shaping of the strap.

1 TO MAKE UP Join the sole and upper seams along the centre back. With orange yarn make a small loop at the end of the ankle strap and work buttonhole stitch into the loop.

2 Fold the T-bar over the ankle strap and sew the end in place on the underside.

3 Sew the button or bead firmly on to the main part of the shoe.

Tasselled Hat

This child's hat is very straightforward to work, either for the beginner or the more experienced knitter. It is made from the most basic of rectangular shapes and its appeal relies on the dynamic use of colour and the extravagant tassels that add a finishing decorative touch. The size given would fit a toddler, but, once the tension (gauge) has been worked out, it is easy to make the hat larger or smaller. The finished hat measures 35cm (14in) around the ribbed edge.

MATERIALS

Small quantities of double knitting yarn in:
 (A) yellow (B) lime (C) pink (D) bright yellow
 (E) orange (F) turquoise (G) red and (H) purple
Embroidery scissors
Pair each of 3.00mm and 3.50mm knitting needles
Tapestry needle
9cm (3⅓in) piece of cardboard

TENSION GAUGE

Using 3.50mm needles, 21sts and 30 rows measures 10cm (4in).
Using 3.00mm needles and yarn A, cast on 48 sts. Work 10 rows K1, P1 rib.
Change to 3.50mm needles and work the following striped pattern in st st:
6 rows B, 2 rows C
6 rows B, 2 rows D
6 rows B, 2 rows E
6 rows B, 2 rows F
6 rows B, 2 rows G
6 rows B, 2 rows H.
Work a further 2 rows for middle top of hat.
Continue in st st for back of hat:
6 rows F, 2 rows A
6 rows F, 2 rows C
6 rows F, 2 rows G
6 rows F, 2 rows E
6 rows F, 2 rows H
6 rows F, 2 rows B.
Break yarn. Using 3.00mm needles and yarn G, work 10 rows K1, P1 rib. Cast off.

1 TO MAKE THE TASSELS Wind a selection of the yarns used in the hat around the rectangle of cardboard to the required thickness – about eight times for each colour. Knot a length of yarn around the loop and tie tightly.

2 Slip the yarn off the card and, holding the loop firmly at one end, take a needle with yarn through the top of the loop twice and secure. Cut through the other end of the loop, then wind a length of yarn around the tassel 12mm (½in) from the top and tie tightly. Comb to separate the yarn strands. Trim level with sharp scissors.

3 TO MAKE UP Fold the hat in half with right sides facing inwards. Stitch the side seams together and turn to the right side.

4 Attach one tassel securely to each corner.

Fringed Scarf

Most novice knitters start out by making a striped scarf, either for themselves or for their teddy bears. It is still the best way to practise the rudiments of knitting. The yarns for this project are specially chosen in natural tweed-like colours, but knitting a multicoloured scarf can be the ideal way to use up odd balls of wool. A deep fringe gives an attractive finish and can be made to match or contrast with the scarf itself.

The finished scarf measures 25 x 140cm (10 x 55in), but could be made longer or narrower.

MATERIALS
Double knitting yarn in various colours
Pair of 4.00mm knitting needles
20cm (8in) piece of cardboard
Large crochet hook

1 Cast on 50 sts and K each row to end. Work the scarf in random stripes of different widths, joining each new colour at the beginning of a row. The loose ends can be darned in afterwards, or worked in as shown simply by holding them behind the main yarn.

2 Trim the tidied ends close to the work.

3 Cast off loosely when the scarf has reached the desired length. Make the fringe by hooking small hanks of yarn through the finished edges. Wrap the wool about ten times round a rectangle of cardboard and slip off. Insert the crochet hook into the edge of the scarf and draw one end of the loop through the knitting. Pull the other end of the hank through the loop to form a knot. Repeat to the end – about 15 hanks.

4 Cut the looped end to form the fringe and trim carefully so that the edge is even.

Ski Hat

Making a simple garment such as this Nordic-style ski hat in the round, using a circular needle, is much easier than knitting it on two needles. The finished piece has no bulky seams to be joined and all the loose yarn is carried on the inside. The stocking-stitch appearance comes from working in knit stitch only, as the work does not have to be turned at the end of the row. The beginning of each round should be indicated with a stitch marker or a strand of contrasting yarn. The finished hat, which would fit an adult, has a circumference of 63cm (25in). Follow the charts for the Fair Isle stripes in the template section.

MATERIALS

50g (2oz) double knitting yarn each in brown, beige, light grey, cream and dark green
2 x 4.00mm circular needles 60cm (24in) and 40cm (16in) long Tapestry needle

1 TO FINISH OFF Darn in the loose ends and pressing the hat lightly. Make the cord tie by twisting together three 60cm (24in) lengths of wool until they fold back on themselves. Knot the ends together to create a loop. Thread this cord through the eyelet holes in the top of the hat.

2 Make a small tassel by wrapping a 60cm (24in) length of yarn around a 5cm (2in) wide piece of card. Slip the hank through the loop at the end of the cord, stitch in place and trim the ends. Repeat for the other end of the cord.

Cast on 96 sts using brown yarn. Work 21 rows K2, P2 rib in stripes as follows, ensuring that the foundation row has not become twisted around the needle.

Rounds 1 and 2 brown.
Rounds 3 and 4 beige.
* **Round 5** brown.
Round 6 light grey.
Round 7 brown.*
Rounds 8 and 9 green.
Rounds 10-12 repeat from * to *.
Rounds 13 and 14 beige.
Rounds 15 and 16 brown.
Round 17 light grey.
Rounds 18 and 19 green.
Round 20 beige.
Round 21 brown.
Continue in st st:
Rounds 22-24 brown.
Round 25 (K3 brown; K1 beige) to end of round.
Round 26 K1 beige, *(K1 brown, K3 beige) rep from * to last 3sts, K1 brown, K2 beige.
Round 27 beige.
Rounds 28-32 follow charted pattern 1, reading from right to left.
Round 33 beige
Round 34-39 follow pattern 2, using beige background.
Round 40 beige.
Rounds 41 and 45 follow pattern 1.
Round 46 beige.
Round 47 (K1 brown, K1 beige) to end of round.

Round 48 brown.
Rounds 49-55 follow pattern 3.
Rounds 56 and 57 brown.
Rounds 58 and 59 beige.
Round 60 green.
Round 61 and 62 beige.
Round 63 with light grey, K10, K2 tog tbl, K2 tog, *(K20, K2 tog tbl, K2 tog), rep from * 3 times, K10 (88 sts).
Change to smaller needle.
Round 65 with brown, K9 K2 tog tbl, K2 tog *(K18, K2 tog tbl, K2 tog) rep from * 3 times, K9 80sts).
Round 66 beige.
Round 67 with beige, K8, K2 tog tbl, K2 tog, *(K14, K2 tog tbl, K2 tog), rep from * 3 times, K8 (72 sts).
Round 68 light grey.
Round 70 brown.
Round 71 with light grey, K6, K2 tog tbl, K2 tog, *(K1, K2 tog tbl, K2 tog) repeat from * 3 times, K6 (56 sts):
Round 72 with brown (K1, cast off 1) to end.
Round 73 with brown (K1, make 1) to end.
Round 74 brown.
Round 75 cast off.

Purse Bag

The favourite Scandinavian colour combination of red and white is used to dramatic effect for this attractive purse bag. Chenille yarn gives it a rich velvety texture which is complemented by mother-of-pearl buttons. The festive motifs of deer and snowflakes make it ideal for Christmas-time, either as a present in itself or as a special package for a tiny gift. The finished bag measures 16.5 x 12.5cm (6½ x 5in).

MATERIALS
50g (2oz) chenille yarn in red
50g (2oz) chenille yarn in white
Pair of 4.50mm knitting needles
Tapestry needle
2 mother-of-pearl buttons

1 Cast on 33 sts and work in stocking stitch. Follow the charted pattern for 54 rows and cast off.

2 Make the button loops on the bottom edge of the finished piece. Using a tapestry needle threaded with red yarn, work blanket stitch into the first 11 stitches, then make a 2cm (¾in) loop, stitch into the next 9 stitches, make another loop, then work to the end. Fold the work in half, right sides facing, and join the two side seams. Turn the bag to the right side and blanket stitch down each side to tidy.

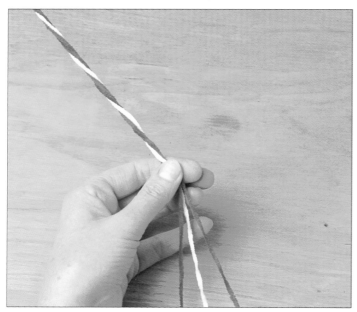

3 Make the cord from two 90cm (36in) lengths of red and one of white yarn. Hold together tightly at one end and twist until the cord folds in half. Make a knot at each end to secure, leaving enough to form a small tassel.

4 Stitch above the knot to fasten the cord to the bag, then sew the two buttons on to the front.

Baby Doll

K nitted toys have a great charm of their own and this engaging baby doll has a very special appeal. He is full of character and certain to delight both adults and children alike. This project is deceptively simple to make: nose, ears, toes, fingers, arms and legs are all knitted separately, using a minimum of shaping, then sewn on to the main body.

MATERIALS
Pair each of 3.00mm and 3.50mm knitting needles
50g (20g) dishcloth yarn (100% pearl cotton)
Oddment of double knitting yarn for the nappy
  (diaper)
Embroidery cotton in black
Washable polyester toy stuffing
Safety pin
Tapestry needle
Pink crayon

BODY AND HEAD
Begin at lower edge of body. Using dishcloth yarn (crochet cotton) and 3.00mm needles, cast on 16 sts.
Row 1 inc k-wise into every st (32 sts).
Starting with a P row, work 19 rows st st.

Shape for head
Next row K6, (K2 tog) 3 times, K8 (K2 tog) 3 times, K6 (26 sts).
Work 13 rows st st.
Dec row (K2 tog) to end – 13 sts.
Break yarn and thread end back through remaining sts.

ARMS
Begin at hand: cast on 5 sts.
Row 1 inc K-wise into every st (10 sts).

Beginning with a P row, work 13 rows st st.
Cast off.

FIRST LEG
Begin at toes: cast on 10 sts, work 6 rows st st.

Shape heel
K5, turn.
Sl 1, P3, turn.
Sl 1, K2, turn.
Sl 1, P1, turn.
Sl 1, K2, turn.
Sl 1, P3, turn.
Sl 1, K4 turn.
Sl 1, P5 turn.
Continuing in st st, work 14 rows. Cast off.

SECOND LEG
Work as given for first leg, but decrease for heel on last 5 sts on needle instead of first.

EARS
Cast on 3 sts, K1 row. Cast off P-wise. Tie ends of yarn together to form ear shape.

NOSE
Cast on 3 sts. Cast off. Tie ends together to form a small round shape.

BIG TOE
Work 2, as for nose.

LITTLE FINGER
Cast on 2 sts. Cast off.

THUMB AND TWO MEDIUM-SIZED FINGERS
Cast on 3 sts. Cast off.

MIDDLE FINGER
Cast on 4 sts. Cast off.

NAPPY (DIAPER)
Using textures DK yarn and 3.50mm needles, cast on 34 sts. K 1 row.
Dec row K2 tog at beg and end of row.
Next row K to end. Rep last 2 rows until 2 sts remain.
Next row K2 tog, thread end through remaining st and secure.

2 ARMS With right sides together, sew the seam lengthways. Turn to the right side and stuff. Tie a length of yarn around the wrist and thread the ends back through the work. Arrange the fingers and thumb and sew to the hand.

1 TO MAKE UP BODY With right sides together, join the seam. Turn to the right side and stuff firmly. Gather up the stitches around the lower edge and close the gap. Tie a length of yarn firmly around the neck and thread the ends back through the work.

3 Sew the arms on to the body, with the body seam at the centre back.

4 FEET AND LEGS With right sides together, sew the seam lengthways. Turn to the right side and stuff. Tie a length of yarn around the ankle and thread the ends back through the work. Using a length of dishcloth yarn (100% pearl cotton), sew back and forth through the work near the end of the foot to form toes.

5 Attach the big toe to the end of the foot and sew the legs to the body. Shape the bottom by stitching through the lower part of the body.

TUMMY BUTTON Work a vertical back stitch just below the centre of the tummy.

6 FACE Attach the ears and nose. Work the eyes and mouth in straight stitch, using a single strand of black embroidery cotton. Lightly colour in the cheeks, the end of the nose, the knees and tummy button with a soft pink crayon.

HAIR Sew small loops of black cotton through the head and knot firmly, then clip to form tufts. With a pink crayon lightly colour in the cheeks, the end of the nose, the knees and the tummy button.

NAPPY (DIAPER) Fold on the nappy (diaper) and fasten with a safety pin. If the doll is intended for a child, the nappy (diaper) should be secured in place with a few stitches instead.

Crochet

An amazing range of crocheted items – from chunky hats to delicate lace – can be produced with just a hook and yarn. The versatility of crochet has been exploited by international fashion designers, and crocheted garments are included in many collections. The basic stitches can be adapted to many uses, and unconventional materials, such as raffia or strips of torn cloth, bring a new dimension to a well-known craft.

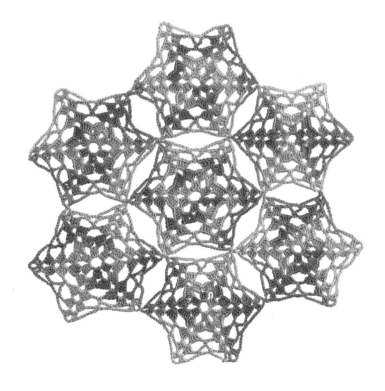

Flower Box

Crochet is a very versatile textile medium. Its use need not be limited to wool and cotton yarns, nor only to two-dimensional objects. In fact, with a little imagination and the creative use of brightly coloured raffia, for example, an empty circular Camembert cheese box can be transformed into the cheerful flower-shaped container shown here.

MATERIALS
1 hank each 2 colours raffia for lid and sides
Small quantities of raffia in various colours for the petals
3.50mm crochet hook
Round cardboard box with lid, approximately
  11.5cm (4½in) in diameter
Pencil; silver foil; tape measure; pva adhesive
Sharp large-eyed needle
Sticky tape

1 The box base and lid are both covered with silver foil, which has been crumpled and straightened out again for a textured effect. Draw around the lid on to the foil, add 5cm (2in) all round and cut out the circle. Snip from the outside edge to the inner circle every 10mm (³⁄₈in), then glue to the top of the box lid, folding and sticking the tabs around both sides of the rim. Draw around the base twice, add a 4cm (1½in) allowance and cut out the two circles. Cut tabs as before, then stick one circle to the inside of the box and one to the outside, to cover entirely.

2 With one of the main colours of raffia, work the box lid:
Round 1 3ch, sl st into 1st ch to form ring. 1 ch, 6 dc into ring, sl st into 1st dc at beg of round.
Round 2 1 ch, 2 dc into each of next 6 sts, sl st into 1st dc at beg of round.
Round 3 1 ch, * (1 dc into 1st st, 2 dc into next st) rep from * to end, sl st into 1st dc at beg of round.
Round 4 1 ch, 1 dc, into each st to end of round, sl st into 1st dc at beg of round. Repeat rounds 3 and 4 three more times.
Round 11 1 ch, 1 dc into each of next 60 sts, sl st into 1st dc at beg of round.
Change to green raffia and work the sides as follows:
Round 12 working into the back loop of each st, work 1 ch, * (1 dc into each of next 14 sts, miss 1 st), rep from * 3 times. Sl st into 1st dc at beg of round.
Round 13 1 ch, 1 dc into each of next 56 sts, sl st in 1st dc at beg of round.
Repeat round 13 once more, or until the sides are the same depth as the box. Finish off, leaving a 90cm (36in) end for sewing.
Make the crochet base using the other main raffia colour and repeat rounds 1-10. Miss round 11 and continue with rounds 12 and 13. Finish off, leaving a long end of raffia.

3 Stretch the crochet raffia over the box lid. Using the raffia length, overstitch the cover to the rim. Attach the crochet base to the main box with running stitch. The crochet should reach only halfway up the sides so that the lid will fit.

4 Crochet the petals around the box lid, using a different colour for each petal as follows: With the inside of box facing, join raffia on to last pink round and work 1 sl st into each of next 5 sts, 1 ch, turn box so that right side is facing. Working back over previous row, 1 dc and 1 htr into 1st st. 2 tr into 2nd st, 2 dtrs into 3rd and 4th sts, 2 trs into 5th st, 1 htr and 1 dc into last st. * ch, turn box around, 1 sl st into each of next 12 sts on previous row, finish off thread.
Working anti-clockwise, with inside of box facing, start the next petal in the stitch on the left of first. Repeat until ten petals have been made. Sew all the ends through to the inside of the box.

5 Make a centre pull for the box lid: 4 ch, sl st into 1st ch to form ring, 1 ch, 10 dc into ring, sl st into 1st dc at beg of round. Finish off, leaving a long end to stitch on to the centre of the lid. Sew the loose ends through to the inside of the lid. Work 8 straight stitches, each in a different colour, around the pull. Trim and tape down the ends inside the box lid and cover with a circle of foil-covered cardboard.

Fabric Bag

This country-style bag uses a technique adapted from rag-rug making, and is crocheted from torn strips of recycled fabric. It is a practical way to use up dressmaking remnants, or to give a second life to the material from an old garment. Cotton or cotton-mix materials provide the best textures. The fabric strips do not have much "give", unless they are cut on the bias, so it is essential to keep the tension loose when working.

MATERIALS

3m (3¼yd) assorted patterned cotton fabric
10.00mm crochet hook
Matching cotton sewing thread; needle

1 Tear the cloth into 12mm (½in) strips, join them together with a few machine or hand stitches and roll each colour into a ball. Make stripes by changing fabric colours as you would if using yarn.

Round 1 Make 4 ch. 1 standing ch, 1 dc in each of 3 ch, 4 dc into 4th ch. On other side of 4 ch make 2 dc, 3 dc in 4th ch. Sl st to 1st ch (12 st).

Round 2 1 ch, 1 dc in same place. 2 dc into each of next 11 dc, sl st to 1st ch (24 sts).

Round 3 1 ch, 8 dc, 2 dc into next dc, 1 dc, 2 dc into next dc, 8 dc, 2 dc, into next dc, 1 dc, 2 dc, into next dc, 1 dc, sl st to 1st ch (28 sts).

2 **Round 4** 1 ch, 8 dc, 2 dc into next dc, 1 dc, 2 dc into next dc, 11 dc, 2dc into next dc, 1 dc, 2dc into next dc, 1 dc, sl st to 1st ch (32 sts).

Round 5 1 ch, 9 dc, 2 dc into next dc, 1 dc, 2 dc into next dc, 13 dc, 2 dc into next dc, 1 dc, 2dc into next dc, 2 dc, sl st to 1st ch (36 sts).

Round 6 1 ch, 1 dc into each dc to end, sl st to 1st ch (36 sts).

Round 7 1 ch, 9 dc, 2 dc into next dc, 1 dc, 2 dc, 15 dc, 2 dc into next dc, 1 dc, 2 dc into next dc, 4 dc, sl st to 1st ch (40 sts).

Round 8 1 ch, 1 dc into each dc to end, sl st to 1st ch (40 sts).

Round 9 1 ch, 9 dc, 2 dc into next dc, 1 dc, 2 dc into next dc, 17 dc, 2 dc into next dc, 1 dc 2 dc into next dc, 7 dc, sl st to 1st ch (44 sts).

Round 10 1 ch, 1 dc into each dc to end, sl st to 1st ch (44 sts).

Round 11 1 ch, 9 dc into next dc, 1 dc, 2 dc into next dc, 19 dc, 2 dc into next dc, 1 dc, 2 dc into next dc, 9 dc, sl st to 1st ch (48 sts).

Round 12 1 ch, 1 dc into each dc to end, sl st to 1st ch (48 sts).

Round 13 as round 12.

Round 14 1 ch, 9 dc, 2 dc into next dc, 1 dc, 2 dc into next dc, 21 dc, 2 dc into next dc, 1 dc, 2 dc into next dc, 11 dc, sl st to 1st ch (52 sts).

Round 15 1 ch, 1 dc into each dc to end, sl st to 1st ch (52 sts).

Round 16 as round 15.

Round 17 1 ch, 1 dc into next 9 dc, 2 dc into next dc, 1 dc, 2 dc into next dc, 23 dc, 2 dc into next dc, 1 dc, 2 dc into next dc, 13 dc, sl st to 1st ch (56 sts).

Round 18 1 ch, 1 dc into each dc to end, sl st to 1st ch (56 sts).

Round 19 as round 18.

Round 20 1 ch, 9 dc, 2 dc into next dc, 1 dc, 2 dc into next dc, 25 dc, 2 dc into next dc, 1 dc, 2 dc into next dc, 15 dc, sl st to 1st ch (60 sts).

Round 21 1 ch, 1 dc into each dc to end, sl st to 1st ch (60 sts).

Round 22 as round 21.

Round 23 1 ch, 9 dc, 2 dc into next dc, 1 dc, 2 dc into next dc, 27 dc, 2 dc into next dc, 1 dc, 2 dc into next dc, 17 dc, sl st to 1st ch (64 sts).

Round 24 1 ch, 1 dc into each dc, sl st to 1st ch (64 sts).

Round 25 as round 24.
Finish off.

3 To make the handles, join the fabric to the top edge of the bag, one-third of the way along from the right-hand side. Make 37 chains and join on to the top edge one-third away from the left-hand side. Turn, and work 1 dc into each chain. Cut off the short end and, with a needle and thread, stitch the fabric securely to the inside of the bag. Repeat on the other side for the second handle.

Baby Blanket and Woollen Balls

This blanket would brighten any nursery and the rainbow colours make it a perfect present for a baby girl or boy. The dramatic chevron pattern is a variation of basic treble stitch, and is quick and easy to work. The matching balls are a good way to use up leftover wool, and can be made in any combination of stripes. They are stuffed with washable polyester fibre, but could be filled with dried beans to make juggling balls for an older child – or adult – to play with. The finished blanket measures about 90cm (36in) square.

BABY BLANKET MATERIALS
50g (2oz) baby double knitting yarn each in red, salmon pink, yellow, green, light blue, dark blue and purple
3.50mm crochet hook
Tapestry needle

1 With red yarn, make a foundation row of 153 ch.
Row 1 Make 1 tr into 4th ch from hook. Make 7 tr into next 7 ch. Into next 3 sts *(yoh [yo], insert hook into ch, draw yarn through, yoh [yo], draw through 2 loops leaving last loop on hook). Repeat from * twice more (4 loops on hook) yoh [yo] and draw through all 4 loops. 13-treble cluster (3 tr cluster) made. 9 tr, 3 tr into next ch, 9 tr*.

2 Repeat from * to * 7 times to end of row. On final repeat work last 2 tr into same ch, turn.
Row 2 3 ch, 1 tr into 1st of 3 ch made, i.e. 2 sts in same place. Work 7 tr. *(1 tr cluster, 9 tr, 3 tr into next tr, 9 tr). Repeat from * to end of row, working last 2 tr into same tr, turn. Repeat row 2 to form the pattern.

Break off the red wool and join the salmon pink wool to the beginning of row for the second stripe.

3 Work two rows of each colour in the spectrum sequence: yellow, green, light blue, dark blue, purple, and repeat the seven-stripe pattern four times, finishing off with an extra two rows of red.

4 Darn in the loose ends of wool. Press the blanket lightly into shape using a damp cloth and cool iron.

WOOLLEN BALL
MATERIALS
*Remnants of double
knitting yarn
3.50mm crochet hook
Washable polyester toy
filling (batting)
Tapestry needle*

1 Make a
foundation
row of 16 ch.
Row 1 1 ch, skip
1 ch, 4 dc, 8 tr, 4
dc, turn.
Row 2 1 ch, 4
dc into next 4 dc,
8 tr into 8 tr, 4
dc into 4 dc turn.

2 These two rows form
the basic pattern and
are repeated nine times to
form the ball shape. A plain
ball can be worked just in
one colour, but changing
yarn at the beginning of
each or every alternate row will create interesting patterns.
The top of the tomato variation is worked in double crochet.

3 Use a tapestry needle to gather the two edges together,
making sure that all the loose ends of yarn are pushed to
the inside of the ball.

4 Sew the edges together with a neat overstitch, to
halfway down the seam. Stuff firmly with polyester
filling (batting), then complete the seam and finish off the
end of the yarn. Roll the ball into shape between your hands.

Strawberry and Tomato Hats

These charming fruit-inspired baby hats could not fail to delight both youngsters and their parents. Stem, calyx and the main part are worked all in one piece, in the round, and the strawberry seeds are embroidered in thick cotton thread. The same pattern is followed for the tomato variation, which is made in a warmer shade of red. The finished hat measures 35cm (14in) around the outer edge and will fit a child of up to one year old.

MATERIALS

Cotton double knitting yarn:
  50g (2oz) in red
  20g (¾oz) in green
  10g (¼oz) in black
  10g (¼oz) in yellow
3.50mm and 4.50mm crochet hook
Large-eyed needle

1 Using green yarn and a 4.50mm hook, make 5 ch.1 sl st in 2nd ch from hook. * sl st in each of 3 remaining ch to form the stem.

Round 1 3 ch, sl st into 1st ch to form a ring. 1 ch, 5 dc into ring, sl st into 1st dc at beg of round.

Round 2 1 ch, 2 dc into each of next 5 sts. Sl st into 1st dc.

Round 3 1 ch, (1 dc in 1st st, 2 dc in next st) 4 times, sl st into 1st dc.

Round 4 1 ch, (1 dc in each of next 2 sts, 2 dc in next st) 4 times, sl st into 1st dc.

Round 5 1 ch, (1 dc in each of next 3 sts, 2 dc in next st) 4 times, sl st into 1st dc.

Round 6 1 ch, (1 dc into each of next 4 sts, 2 dc into next st) 4 times, sl st into 1st dc (30 sts).

2 Work the leaves as follows:
Round 7 *(12 ch, 1 sl st into 2nd ch from hook, 1 sl st into next ch, 1 dc into each of next 2 ch, 1 htr into each next 2 ch, 1 tr into each of next 2 ch, 1 dtr into each of next 3 ch. Join leaf to hat with a sl st into the front loop only of 4th st from beg of 12 ch, 1 sl st into the front loop of next st). Repeat from * 5 times.

3 Change to red and, working into the back loop of each st in the previous row, make 1 ch (1 dc into each of the next 5 sts, 2 dc into next st) 4 times, sl st into 1st dc at beg of round.

Round 8 1 ch (1 dc into each of next 6 sts, 2 dc in next st) 4 times, sl st into 1st dc.

Round 9 1 ch, (1 dc in each of next 7 sts, 2 dc into next st) 4 times, sl st into 1st dc.

Round 10 1 ch, (1 dc into each of next 8 sts, 2 dc into next st) 4 times, sl st into 1st dc.

Round 11 1 ch, (1 dc into each of next 9 sts, 2 dc into next st) 4 times, sl st into 1st dc.

Round 12 1 ch, (1 dc into each of 1st 10 sts, 2 dc into next st) 4 times, sl st into 1st dc.

Round 13 1 ch, 1 dc into each of 60 sts, sl st into 1st dc. Repeat round 13, 13 more times to row 27.

4 **Round 27** change to 3.50mm hook and work 2 ch, 1 tr into same st, 1 tr into each of next 59 sts, sl st into 1st tr. Fasten off and sew in all ends of yarn.

5 If making the strawberry hat, embroider the seeds with black yarn. Work each one with a daisy stitch, keeping the floating threads between each stitch on the inside of the work as short as possible. Complete by making a small straight stitch in yellow in the centre of each black seed.

Cotton Duffle Bag

This lightweight duffle bag is made in natural unbleached crochet cotton. It can easily be packed away and would make an ideal beach bag for a summer holiday. Two different-sized hooks are used: a 3.50mm to make compact stitches for a firm base and a 4.50mm to achieve a bulkier crunchy effect for the openwork V-stitch sides. The two pieces are crocheted together to make a strong seam which will stand up to hard wear.

The finished bag measures 35cm (14in) deep and 51cm (20in) around the top.

MATERIALS
150g craft cotton
3.50mm and 4.50mm crochet hooks
Tapestry needle

1 BASE With a 3.50mm hook, make 5 ch and join into a ring with a sl st into 1st ch.

Round 1 1 ch, 11 dc into ring, join with sl st to top of 1st ch (12 sts).

Round 2 3 ch (to stand as 1 tr), 1 tr into same place, (1 tr into next dc, 2 tr into next dc) to end of round, sl st to top of 3rd ch at beg of round (18 sts).

Round 3 3 ch, 1 tr into same place, 2 tr into each tr to end of round, sl st to top of 3rd ch (26 sts).

Round 4 3 ch, 1 tr into each tr to end of round, sl st to top of 3rd ch (54 sts).

Round 5 3 ch, (1 tr in each of next 2 tr, 2 tr in next tr), to end of round, sl st to top of 3rd ch (70 sts).

Round 6 3 ch, 1 tr into each tr, to end of round, sl st to top of 3rd ch (70 sts).

Round 7 3 ch, (1tr into next tr, 2 tr into next tr) to end of round, sl st to top of 3rd ch (106 sts).

Round 8 3 ch, 1 tr in each tr to end of round, st st to top of 3 ch, finish off yarn (106 sts).

2 SIDES Using a 3.50mm hook, make 103 ch.
Row 1 1 tr into 4th ch from hook, 1 tr into each ch to end (100 tr), turn.

Row 2 3 ch (to stand as 1 tr), 1 tr into each tr to end (100 tr), turn.

Row 3 repeat row 2.

Row 4 Change to a 4.50mm hook.
4 ch, skip 2 tr (1 dtr, 1 ch, 1 dtr [= 1 V st] into next tr. miss 2 tr, 1 V st into next tr) to end of row, 1 dtr into last st, turn.

Row 5 4 ch (1 V st into 1 V st), repeat to end, 1 dtr into last st, (31 V sts), turn.

Rows 6–21 Repeat row 5, 16 times.

EYELET ROW Change to a 3.50mm hook.
Row 22 1 ch, 1 dc into each st of previous row (95 dc).

Row 23 1 ch, 1 dc into each dc to end (95 dc).

Row 24 3 ch, (1 tr into 1 dc) twice, (2 ch, skip 2 dc, 3 tr into next 3 dc) repeat to end of row, ending with 3 tr.

Row 25 1 ch, 1 dc into each st to end of row.

Row 26 1 ch, 1 dc into each dc to end of row. Finish off.

3 MAKING UP Press all the pieces lightly into shape and darn in any loose ends with a tapestry needle. Join the two short sides of the main bag together with double crochet, then attach the base in the same way to the lower edge of the bag.

SHOULDER STRAPS Using a 3.50mm hook, make 10 ch.
Row 1 make 1 tr in 4th ch from hook, 1 tr in each ch to end (7sts), turn.
Row 2 1 ch, 1 dc into each tr to end (7sts), turn.
Row 3 3 ch, 1 tr into each dc to end (7sts), turn.
Repeat rows 2 and 3 until the strap measures 51cm (20in).

4 Fold the strap in half and stitch securely to the top edge of the bag across the seam. Sew the two ends to the base of the bag as shown. Make a cord from a length of chain stitch or by twisting a long length of yarn back on itself, and thread through the eyelets.

111

Coasters and Placemat

Thick cotton in a subtle range of colours is used to crochet this placemat and coaster set, which makes it both attractive and practical; the yarn is heat-resistant, absorbent and keeps its shape when washed. The rectangular mat is in basketweave pattern. This raised-effect stitch is usually worked in a single colour, but the introduction of stripes gives it an added depth and texture. Making the coasters is a good way to practise crocheting circles; each is made in a different combination of three colours.

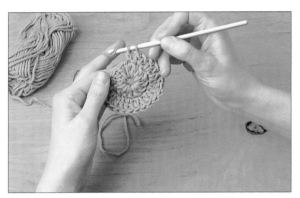

1 COASTERS
With colour 1, make 7 ch and join with sl st to form a circle.
Round 1 3 ch, 14 tr into circle, join with sl st into top of 3 ch.
Round 2 3 ch, 1 tr in same sp, (2 tr into 1 st) to end of round, join with sl st to top of 3 ch, break yarn (28 sts).

2 **Round 3** join colour 2. 3 ch, 1 tr (2 tr into next st, 1 tr) to end of round, join with sl st to top of 3 ch, break yarn (42 sts).
Round 4 join colour 3. 2 ch, 1 htr into each st to end of round, join with sl st to top of 2 ch (42 sts).

3 Finish off, darn in the end and press lightly.

COASTER MATERIALS
50g (2oz) balls of thick cotton yarn each in dark purple, claret, mustard, sage green and sap green
4.50mm crochet hook; large-eyed needle

1 PLACEMAT **Row 1** Using dark purple yarn, make 42 ch. Work 1 tr into 4th ch from hook, then 1 tr into each ch to end of row, turn.
Row 2 3 ch, yoh. Instead of working through loops at top of next tr, insert hook from right to left under the stitch itself, draw yarn through, then complete tr as usual (= 1 raised front treble, rftr). 1 rftr in next tr.

2 The next 3 raised sts are worked in the same way, but the hook is inserted from the back of the work and from right to left under the stitch (= raised back treble, rbtr). Work (3 rftr, 3 rbtr) 5 times to last 3 sts, 3 rftr, turn.
Row 3 3 ch, 2 rftr, (3 rbtr, 3 rftr) 6 times. Break yarn, turn.
Row 4 Join claret yarn and work 3 ch, 2 rftr (3 rbtr, 3 frtr) 6 times to end, turn.
Row 5 (3 rftr, 3 rbtr) 6 times to last 3 sts, 3 rftr, break yarn, turn.
These 2 rows form the basketweave pattern.
Continue working in the following stripes:
Rows 6 and 7 mustard
Rows 8 and 9 sage green
Rows 10 and 11 sap green
Rows 12 and 13 sage green
Rows 14 and 15 mustard
Rows 16 and 17 claret
Rows 18 to 20 dark purple.

3 Work the border in sage green. Join the yarn to the edge of the mat at the top right edge and work 1 tr in each st and 3 tr into each corner st. Along the sides, make 3 tr, evenly spaced, into the side of each tr, so that the stitches cover the loose ends of the yarn. Alternately you can darn these in. Darn in the green yarn and press the mat lightly into shape.

PLACEMAT MATERIALS
50g (2oz) balls of thick cotton yarn each in dark purple, claret, mustard, sage green and sap green
4.00mm crochet hook; large-eyed needle

Templates

This section gives all the patterns, charts and templates needed for making the step-by-step projects. Many of them have been reduced and can be increased to the size required by using a photocopier. Alternatively, the grid outlines can be used as a guide for enlarging by hand.

To enlarge the patterns shown on grids, find or draw onto paper a grid of 1in (25mm) squares. Taking one square at a time, copy the lines of the pattern onto your full-size grid. This will give an actual-size pattern.

Embroidery – Alphabet Sampler

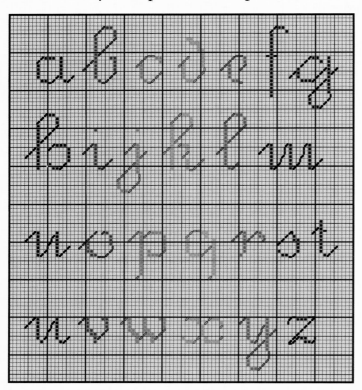

Embroidery – Cross Stitch Motifs

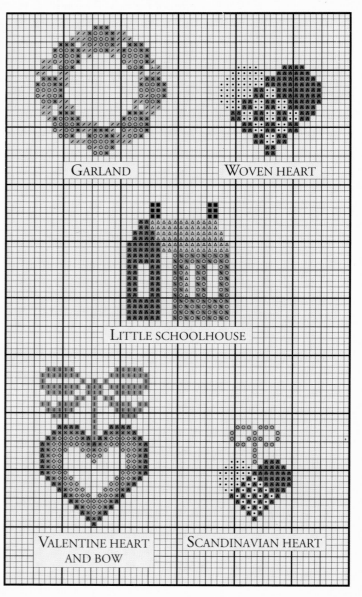

GARLAND

WOVEN HEART

LITTLE SCHOOLHOUSE

VALENTINE HEART
AND BOW

SCANDINAVIAN HEART

Embroidery – Potpourri Bag

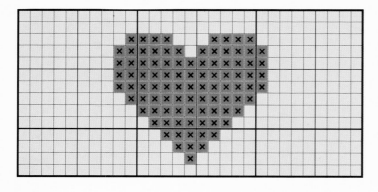

Embroidery – Fabric Book

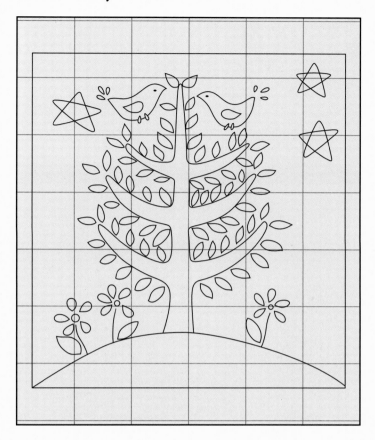

Embroidery – Tea Towel

Embroidery –
House and Garden Picture

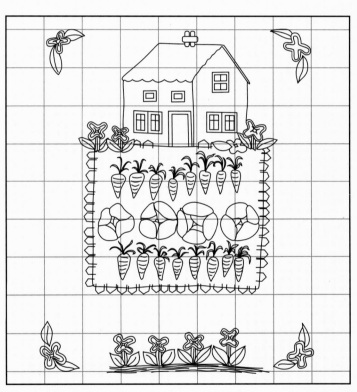

Embroidery – Rocket Bag

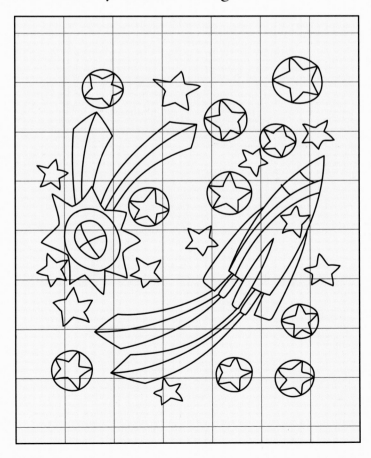

Embroidery – Folk Art Gloves

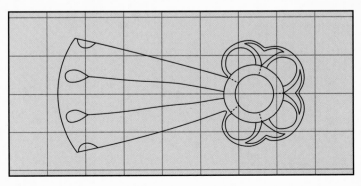

Embroidery – Hairslide (Barrette)

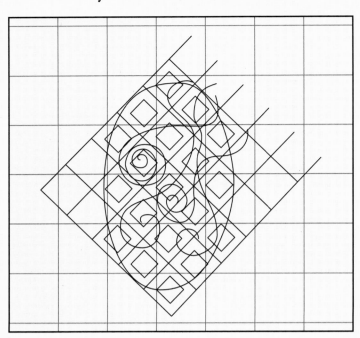

Embroidered – Hat

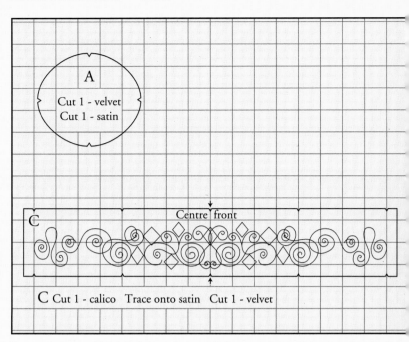

Embroidery – Picture Frame

Embroidery – Drawstring Bag

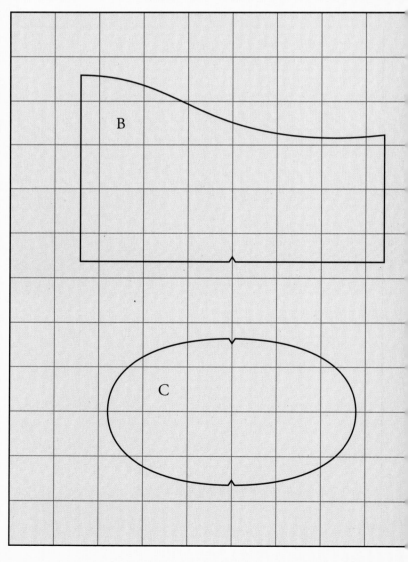

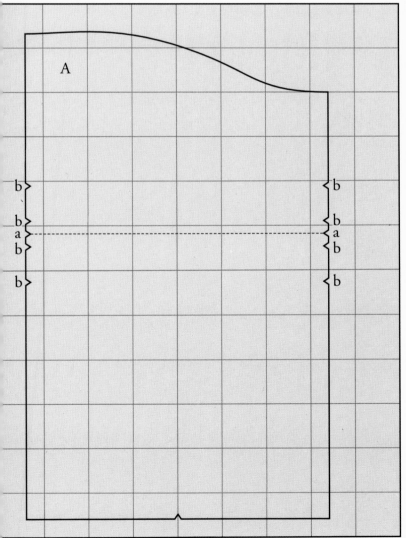

B

Cut 1 - velvet
Cut 1 - satin

1.5CM (⅝IN) SEAM ALLOWANCE INCLUDED

A

b
b
a b
b

b
b
a b
b

b

b

Embroidery – Placemat

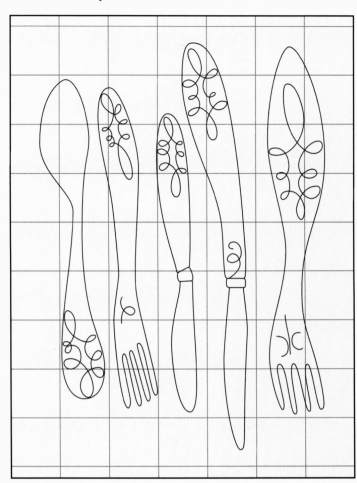

Embroidery – Cat Picture

Embroidery – Fish Mobile

Embroidery – Table Cloth

Needlepoint – Jewellery Box

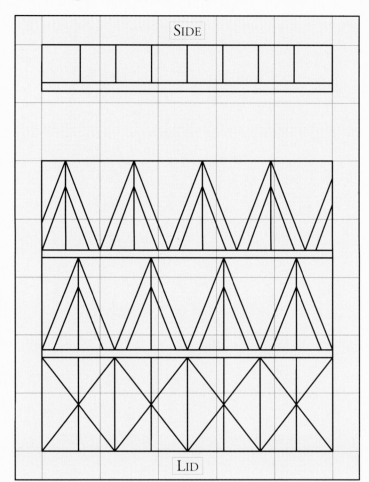

Needlepoint – Lone-star Cushion (Pillow)

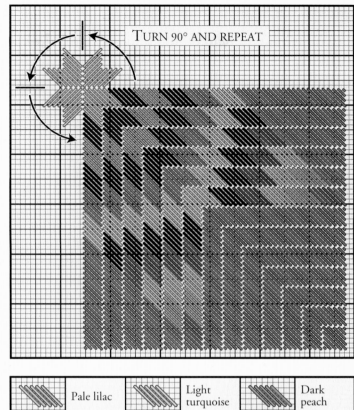

	Pale lilac		Light turquoise		Dark peach
	Dark purple		Crimson		Orange
	Indigo		Dark turquoise		Dark gold

Needlepoint – Nine-star Cushion (Pillow)

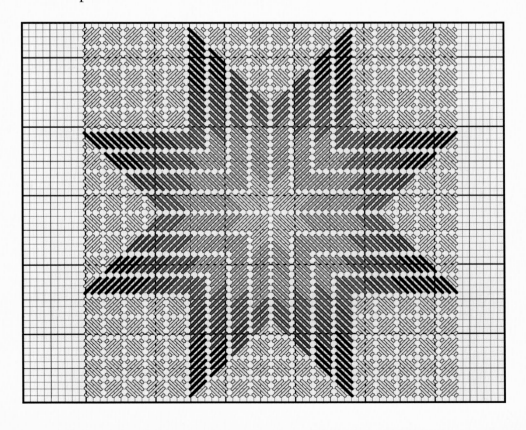

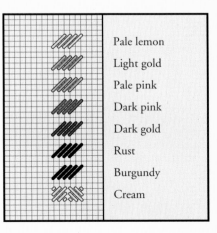

	Pale lemon
	Light gold
	Pale pink
	Dark pink
	Dark gold
	Rust
	Burgundy
	Cream

Needlepoint – Heart Picture

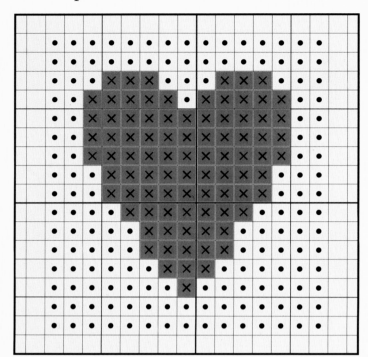

Needlepoint – Circular Star

Needlepoint – Cup and Saucer

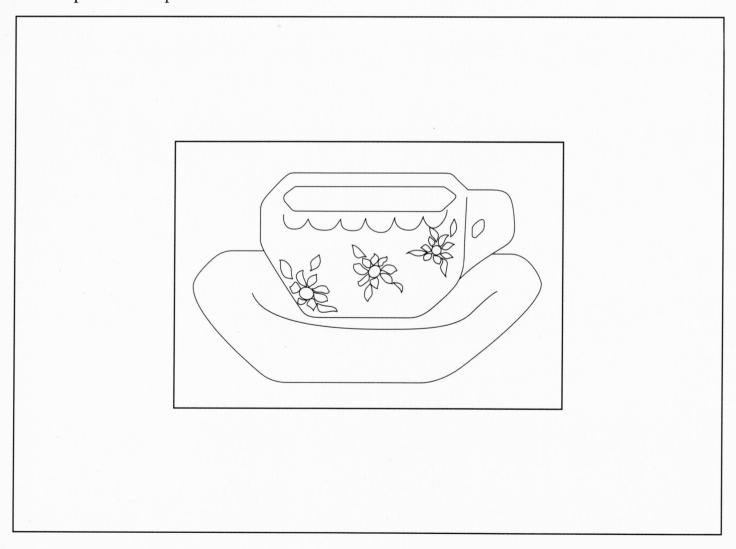

Needlepoint – Sun Pincushion

Needlepoint – Brooch Cushion (Pillow)

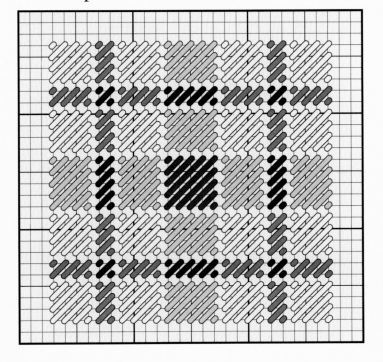

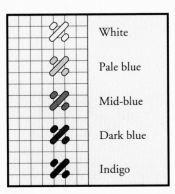

White

Pale blue

Mid-blue

Dark blue

Indigo

Needlepoint – Needle Book

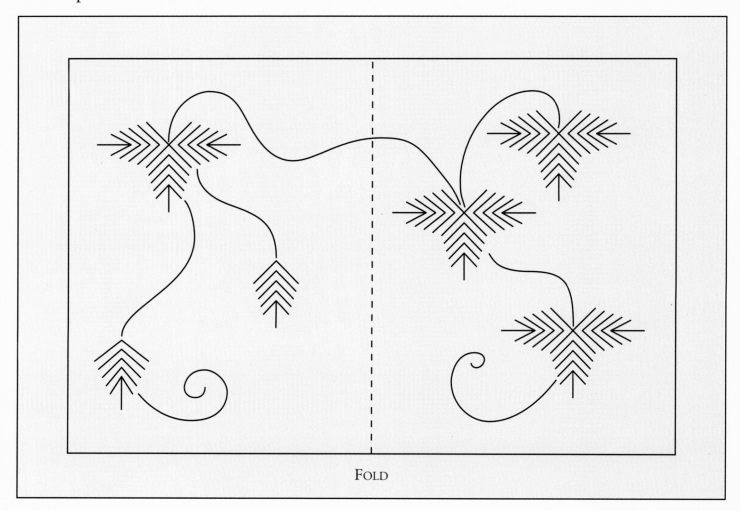

FOLD

Needlepoint – Scissor Case

Patchwork – Red Star

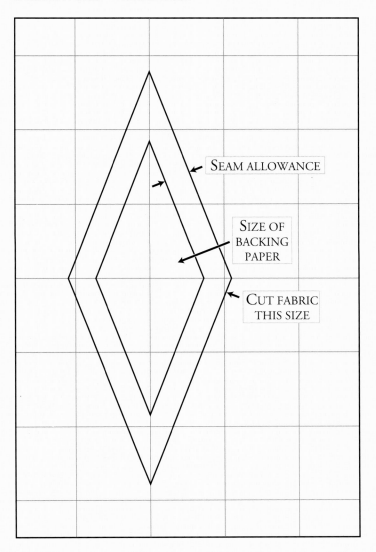

SEAM ALLOWANCE

SIZE OF
BACKING
PAPER

CUT FABRIC
THIS SIZE

Patchwork – Saw-tooth Star Bag

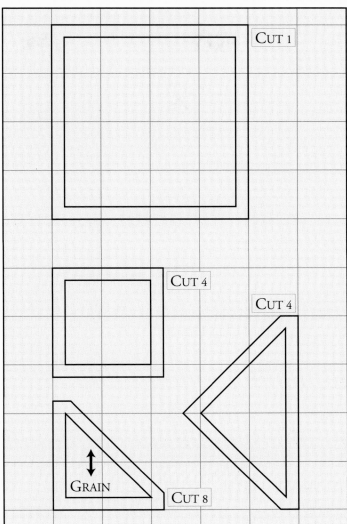

CUT 1

CUT 4

CUT 4

GRAIN

CUT 8

Patchwork – Log-cabin Yarn Roll

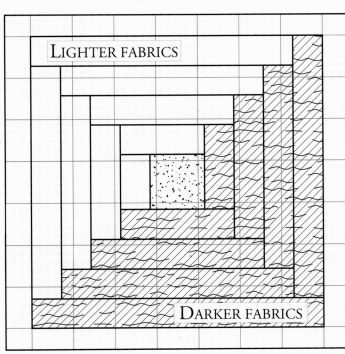

LIGHTER FABRICS

DARKER FABRICS

Patchwork – Heart Cushion (Pillow)

Appliqué – Star-fruit Panel

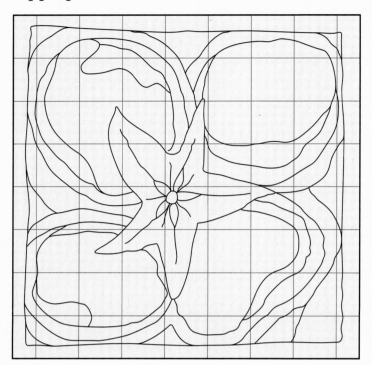

Appliqué – Cornucopia

Appliqué – Oven Glove (Mitt)

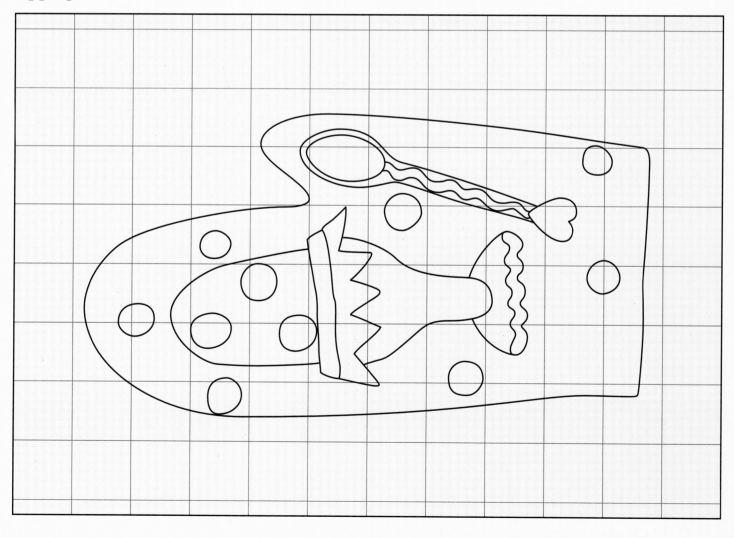

Appliqué – Goose Shopping Bag

Appliqué – Apron

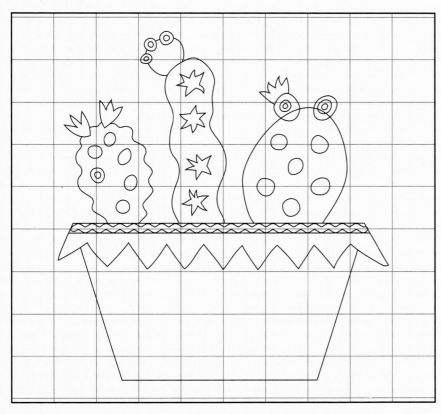

Appliqué – Bolster Pillow

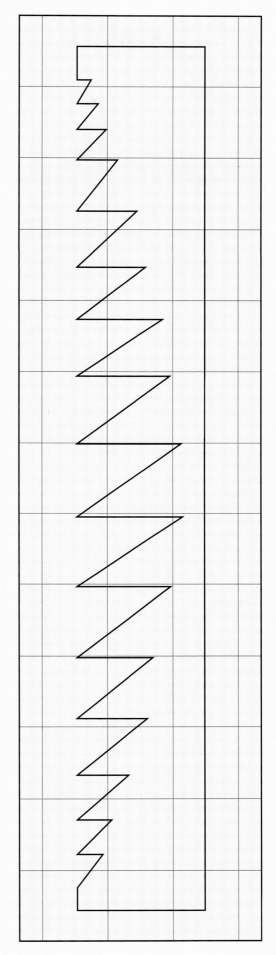

Knitting – Baby Wrap

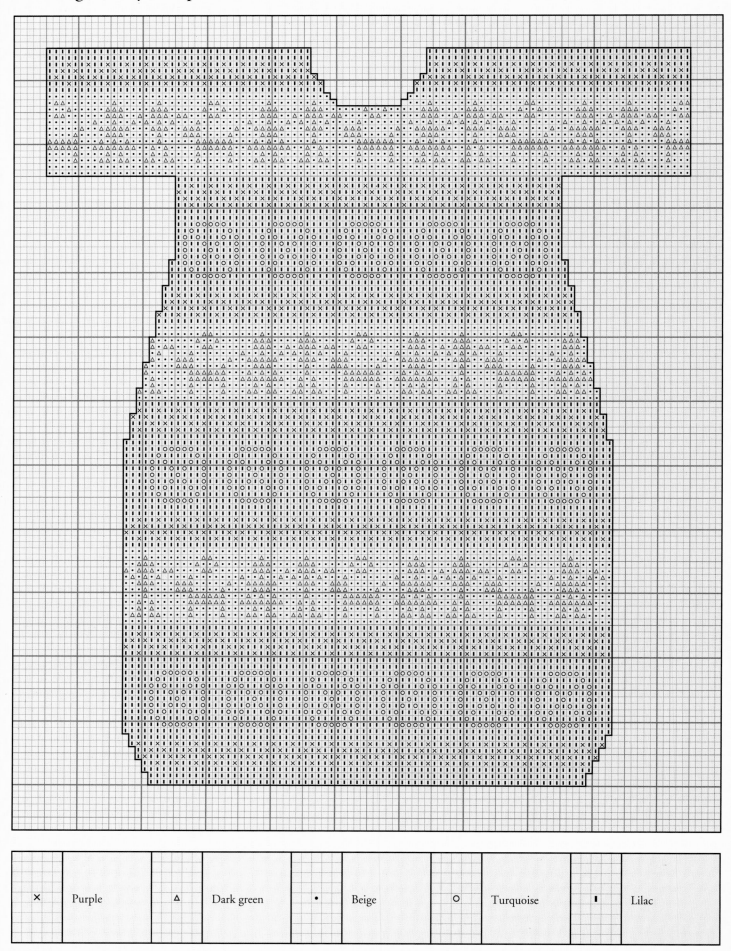

×	Purple	△	Dark green	•	Beige	○	Turquoise	ı	Lilac